LEADERSHIP
SECRETS
OF THE
WORLD'S
MOST
SUCCESSFUL
CEOS

LEADERSHIP
SECRETS
OF THE
WORLD'S
MOST
SUCCESSFUL
CEOs

ERIC YAVERBAUM

Dearborn™
Trade Publishing
A **Kaplan Professional** Company

Vice President and Publisher: Cynthia A. Zigmund
Acquisitions Editor: Jonathan Malysiak
Senior Project Editor: Trey Thoelcke
Interior Design: Lucy Jenkins
Cover Design: Scott Rattray, Rattray Design
Typesetting: Elizabeth Pitts

© 2004 by Eric Yaverbaum

Published by Dearborn Trade Publishing
A Kaplan Professional Company

Printed in the United States of America

04 05 06 10 9 8 7 6 5 4 3 2 1

Library of Congress Cataloging-in-Publication Data

Yaverbaum, Eric.
    Leadership secrets of the world's most successful CEOs / Eric Yaverbaum.
        p.   cm.
Includes index.
    ISBN 0-7931-8061-9
    1. Leadership. 2. Executive ability. 3. Chief executive officers. 4. Industrial
management. I. Title.
HD57.7.Y38   2004
658.4′092—dc22

                                                                          2003022995

DEDICATION

To Suri, Cole, and Jace

All we ever need is in our own backyard.

"I consider my life, primarily, to be a continuing education course, and I am looking forward to learning more before the day is over."
—Ted Turner, quoted in *Rochester Review,* Winter 2002-2003, p. 3.

Contents

First and foremost I have to thank the best writer to walk the planet—the only writer I would ever collaborate on books with, and a man I have come to have the greatest of personal and professional respect for—Bob Bly.

I cannot thank Maryann Palumbo enough for introducing me to my super agent, Bob Diforio, who found a great home for this book, and my editor Trey Thoelcke for making the manuscript much better than it was when it first crossed his desk. Major thanks to Jonathan Malysiak for his advice and wisdom in bringing the book to Dearborn.

I want to thank the Young Presidents Organization, which I have been a very active member of, for the great inspiration it's members have given to me over the last decade and the main reason I have become so fascinated with the topic of leadership.

I remain deeply appreciative to key members of my public relations agency, Jericho Communications, who are always so supportive while I add the responsibility of "author" to my already complicated day. No doubt it makes the day a little harder for them. Thanks to my long-time partner Jonathan Sawyer and parts of my wonderful staff and associates, including Ian Madover, Kathy Bell, Tara McNally, Greg Mowery, Felicitas Pardo, Kevin DeSantis, Alison DeSena, Cindy Gittelsohn, Julie Lin, Michelle Mandara, Vanessa Losada, Susan McGill, Alyson Herman, Diane Shillingford, Ian McRae, Dominic Park, Karine Ng, Novel Sholars, Daniel Teboul, Jessica Schaifer, Zahya Hantz, Jessica Greenberg, Ana DaSilva, Sharifa Mills, Chris Roberts, Aline Khatchadourian, and Aki Hakuta. A particularly big thank you to Michelle Frankfort for her work on the IKEA chapter. A very, very special thank you to Ursula Cuevas, who spent an awful lot of time keeping all of this organized for me.

Thanks to all the executives who took time out of their enormously busy schedules to be interviewed for this book. Thanks also to the public relations professionals and communications managers who made these interviews happen on time.

Thanks to my in-laws, Bernie and Noreen Nisker, for all their help on the homefront while I was busy writing. And as always to my mother and father Harry and Gayle who support any and everything I do.

Who knows what it really takes to be an effective leader in the business world? The world's most successful CEOs, of course, the men and women who run the #1 or #2 corporation in their industry or market niche.

The idea for this book came to me at a dinner I had a couple of years ago with a small group of CEOs and Richard Grasso, former head of the New York Stock Exchange. The conversation between Mr. Grasso and the other CEOs about leadership during 9/11 made it crystal clear how many brilliant and varied ways there are to be a great leader.

If that evening could have been videotaped and people could have watched the conversations, you could have picked up dozens of leadership strategies from some of the world's most successful men and women. I realized that no one leader has all the answers, but if you combined the most brilliant ones, you'd have everything you need to lead your organization to success.

In *Leadership Secrets of the World's Most Successful CEOs*, 100 top CEOs reveal—in their own words and through exclusive interviews not published elsewhere—their secrets of effective leadership: the proven strategies, attitudes, behaviors, philosophies, and tactics they have used to help themselves and their organizations rise to the top.

But can they really teach you to do what they do? Can leadership be learned? "Leadership is not an innate characteristic, and it can be developed through training," notes Garee Earnest, Ph.D., of Ohio State University. An article in *The Wall Street Journal* says, "Are leaders born or can they be made? Increasingly, experts say the latter."

According to *The Wall Street Journal Career Journal*, a survey of 300 company presidents and CEOs found that these executives believe they were born with only 40 percent of their leadership abilities. The remaining 60 percent they developed through experiences.

Other studies, such as Daniel Goleman's book *Primal Leadership: Realizing the Power of Emotional Intelligence* (Harvard Business School Press, 2002), indicate that an individual's ability to recognize and regulate his emotions, and the emotions of others, accounts for 80 percent of leadership success in organizations. An article in *ComputerWorld* magazine concludes, "Leadership qualities can be spotted and nurtured, and everyone has leadership potential."

To find out the *Leadership Secrets of the World's Most Successful CEOs,* we interviewed more than a hundred CEOs and simply asked them three critical questions:

What is your most powerful leadership technique?

Can you give one or two examples of how this technique increased profitability, helped you gain market share, or achieved another important objective for your company?

How can a person become a better leader?

Then we edited each interview into a short summary and explanation of that CEO's most powerful "leadership secret." Reading time: less than seven minutes each.

The recognition of the importance of leadership skills in business—and the demand for leadership information—is growing. According to an article in *Executive Leadership* newsletter, 40 percent of U.S. corporations now have some sort of formal leadership-training program. A recent Harris Poll shows that only a third of senior management of Fortune 500 companies feel confident in the abilities of the next generation of leaders.

Recent newspaper stories about Enron, WorldCom, Tyco, ImClone, Arthur Anderson, Martha Stewart, and Global Crossing have dramatized the current leadership crisis in corporate America today. In fact, the number of CEOs ousted for poor performance has increased 130 percent over the past six years. Clearly, thousands of businesspeople in these companies and others—from shop floor supervisors to presidents—could benefit from the management and leadership strategies and ideas shared in this book.

I do have one favor to ask. If you have a leadership technique that has been particularly effective for you, why not send it to me so I can share it with readers of future editions of this book? You will receive full credit, of course. Simply e-mail: eric@jerichopr.com.

1

GENE A. ABBOT, CEO

Abbott and Associates, Inc.

A good leader makes sure he is surrounded by the right people.

"Success is not achieved totally by leadership alone," says Gene Abbot, CEO of contracting firm Abbott and Associates. "A good leader makes sure he is surrounded by the right people, that there are open lines of communication in all matters, and that there is a strong commitment by all.

"I have been a mechanical contractor for 34 years. One of our more prominent projects was the TARP project, better known as The Deep Tunnel, for the Metropolitan Sanitary District of Greater Chicago.

"The project was 300 feet below grade level, and all of our heating and cooling equipment and material had to be lowered to that level. It was to be installed, at an elevation of 55 feet, in an equipment room the size of a football field.

"I received a call that we had a serious problem. The room was equipped with a permanently installed overhead crane, which was in the way of our scaffolding.

"After several meetings, we were able to convince the tunnel coordinators of the necessity to build an extension platform from the overhead crane. We then used this platform to assemble and install our equipment above the elevation of the crane. Through leadership, communication, and dedication, we took a critical situation and turned it into a positive result that was appreciated by all.

"Another significant project for us was the Argonne National Laboratory in Lemont, Illinois. The facility is for scientific use and has a one-and-a-half mile circumference.

"Our contract was for $6 million. Once the project got underway, there were interferences due to design and having available access to move productivity.

"Through our communication, leadership, and dedication, our team managed to take 13 sections of this facility and orchestrate them as one typical section. This process allowed us to fabricate all the material on a typical basis, to be aggressive, and to have the material already in place before the facility was even roofed.

"The Argonne people were awed by our hard work and dedication to be so far in advance of the project schedule. In fact, we were recognized and thanked personally for our performance, not only for our work on the project, but also for the safety that was instilled. Argonne prepared a safety video, using our personnel's performance and exhibits, which was mailed to every Argonne facility in the world."

Gene's conclusion: "Only through one's willingness and dedication to give one's self, and strive solely to be the best, not the biggest, can one become a better leader."

2

DANIEL P. AMOS, CEO
AFLAC

Treat your employees well.

"I have a simple management philosophy," says Dan Amos, CEO of insurance giant AFLAC. "If you treat your employees well, they will take care of your customers and your business.

"Our first job is to take care of our employees. They, in turn, have always taken care of our business.

"Our employees know that we listen to and value their ideas, no matter how foreign they may seem to us at first. As a result, our employees extend the same courtesy to our customers. By appreciating the different viewpoints of our employees and customers, we have developed stronger products, new customers, and long-term relationships with policyholders."

According to Dan, AFLAC is the largest foreign life insurer in Japan, in terms of profits, and the second most profitable foreign company in any industry. In 1998 AFLAC was ranked the #1 insurance company in *Fortune* magazine's list of the 100 Best Companies to Work for in America, and was included in the overall listing for the fifth consecutive year.

In February 2003, for the third consecutive year, *Fortune* named AFLAC as one of America's Most Admired Companies in the life and health insurance industry. In July 2002, *Fortune* named AFLAC to its list of America's 50 Best Companies for Minorities. Additionally, AFLAC is a component of the Standard & Poor's 500 Index and has received an A+ (Superior) rating from AM Best.

"Our success is no accident," says Dan. "It is a direct result of our people-first management philosophy and the business strategy we have pursued for many years.

"We identify consumer needs and develop affordable products to meet those needs. We create marketing initiatives that help our sales associates sell our products. And, when a customer becomes a claimant, we honor our commitments by paying claims quickly and fairly.

"Keeping the promises we make to customers is the most important aspect of our success, and our ability to do that depends on the positive relationships our employees build with our customers. That's why we keep our employees foremost in our thinking.

"We want AFLAC to be a company that is known as much for the strength of its character as it is for the strength of its financial performance. Continuing the success that we have enjoyed depends on our ability to nurture and listen to the many voices that comprise our employees, our communities, our customers, and our business partners. I believe that seeking out and engaging the diverse talents and perspectives of our employees produce better decisions for the company, which, in turn, produce better bottom-line results.

"For example, years ago employees told us that childcare was a big issue for our working parents. In 1991, we opened the Imagination Station, offering day care for children of employees. It was so successful that in 2001, we opened the Imagination Station II. Today, we are the largest childcare provider in Georgia.

"The daycare facilities have helped our working parents better balance their lives. They are better able to concentrate on our customers and their jobs because they know their children are receiving good care. The Imagination Stations are located across the street from our work sites, so working parents can check on their children or visit them for lunch.

"Benefits like the Imagination Station contribute to our ability to retain talented employees. The average tenure of an AFLAC employee is ten years.

"We are also just beginning to see some of the children who grew up at the Imagination Station entering our workforce. These children are an asset to the company. They already know our corporate culture—they know about AFLAC—and are anxious to contribute to the company's success.

"We make sure that all our employees participate in the success or failure of our overall business. Every AFLAC employee gets stock options and all employees are eligible for our yearly profit sharing program.

"Employees have a vested interest in how well we serve our customers. As our business grows, so does their wealth. The profit-sharing bonus is based on both the company's performance and an individual's ability to achieve job-related goals. This means that your colleague's ability to get the job done directly affects your bonus and the value of your stock.

"As a result, we do not hear the phrase 'that's not my job.' Everyone understands that in order for the company to achieve its goals, everyone must work together. These ties build a loyalty and dedication that is made of tough stuff.

"Even when folks leave us, we find they often still remain a part of the AFLAC family. We recently held a state of the company event for our retirees. It was such a big hit that we made it an annual event. Additionally, all retirees receive the company magazine, the AFLAC Family Album.

"All employees are given stock options and most keep their stock even after they leave the company. They remain interested in the company as investors. Many of the employees are second- and third-generation AFLAC employees. They discuss the company at family reunions and with me at the grocery store or in church.

How can a person learn to become a better leader? "My advice to someone who wants to improve their leadership skills is to improve their listening and communications skills.

"I believe that communication is at the heart of good leadership. A good leader communicates the vision and values of the company through his words and actions. He listens to the problems that his employees are facing in executing his vision and makes the necessary adjustments. He cares about his customers' needs and works hard to make sure that the company's products and employees meet those needs.

"A company is a living, breathing organization and in order to successfully lead it, you must always remember that it takes people to buy your products, sell your products, and service your products. It is important that your corporate leaders clearly communicate your commitment, your corporate values, and let each employee know how important his or her role is to the success of the company.

"Being a great communicator requires that you connect with people on a number of levels. You have to understand complicated technical issues, but you have to make sure you can present these issues clearly and understandably to every employee, regardless of their function in the company.

"I use e-mails and handwritten notes to communicate about simple matters and transmit information quickly. I place phone calls and stop by offices for matters that are more complex and require more discussion. When I really need to get a point across in a way that brings attention, I send out a memo. Because memos from me are rare inside AFLAC, they get noticed and acted upon.

"I hold regular staff meetings for my senior managers to discuss issues that impact each of us. AFLAC holds regular State of the Company meetings for employees to let them know how their company is being run. These meetings are any opportunity to help our employees keep the bigger picture in focus, to set the context for everything they do, and explain the complexities that affect our overall business. Most importantly, these meetings are my opportunity to help them understand why each of their roles are important to AFLAC's overall success.

"We have a program called Bright Ideas that allows employees to submit ideas and be rewarded if these ideas are implemented. The *AFLAC Family Album,* our employee magazine, highlights individual contributions to the company.

"AFLAC works hard to foster an environment where people know that we are interested in their ideas and their personal growth. We want them to know that their ideas are welcome, and that we'll implement them, because those good ideas help improve the health of our business.

"At core, communicating should foster a very high level of teamwork and a unified understanding of corporate goals. And if a leader is going to be successful, he has to listen—he has to make sure that he is hearing all of the diverse viewpoints that are present in a big business.

"Finally, a leader has to ask a lot of questions of employees: What motivates them? Which of their needs are being met? Which are not? How can you help them? What impact will helping them have on your business? Listening to and acting on the needs of employees helps our business in the short term and over the long term."

3

WILLIAM BONNER, PRESIDENT

Agora

Focus on the work itself.

When asked to share his most powerful leadership technique, Bill Bonner, founder and president of Agora, a large international publisher of newsletters and other specialized information, replied: "I practice a technique that might be called *dynamic indifference*. I do not try to lead, probably because I am no good at it. Instead, I merely focus on the work itself.

"What needs to be done? Who's got a better idea? Who's going to do it? No attempt is made to lead.

"Just the contrary, people are ignored. Finally, they get tired of being ignored and turn to me for leadership. Then I tell them I can't help them. This forces them to figure out the problem for themselves and resolve it.

"For instance, we had a publication that had been our flagship newsletter but had become very difficult. It was losing money. No one knew quite what to do about it.

"Part of the problem, I realized, was that I was being too much of a leader. People waited for me to lead, to come up with a solution, to tell them what to do.

"So I cleverly abdicated. I said to the team, 'If you want this product to survive, you'd better figure something out yourself. I'm taking myself out of this project.' The young woman who was then the editor took the knife between her teeth and went to work. Within six months the publication was profitable again.

"Our business is an example of what Hayek called a *spontaneous order*. People are brought in because there is work to do. Those who need someone to tell them what to do generally leave after a few months. Others learn pretty quickly that they have to figure it out for themselves.

"In France, for example, we tried telling people what to do—from London, no less. It was a disaster. Then, at the end of our ropes, we told the remaining French employees that they would have to figure it out for themselves. 'Who will be in charge?' they wanted to know. 'Whoever takes charge,' we replied.

"It was chaos for a while. Then, a young guy who is probably a closet Marxist, and who had resisted everything we had tried to do previously, gradually took the bit between his teeth, rallied the others, cut expenses, and seemed to be on his way to figuring out how to run a profitable enterprise. Later, he had what seemed to be a nervous breakdown and it looked like, once again, the company was headed down the tubes. Dynamic indifference doesn't always work. But, it's what you do when you can't do better. And it works amazingly well, amazingly often. After the defection of one of the star members, the surviving members of the management team pulled together and, once again, seem to be staging a comeback.

"For a long time, we thought we were completely alone in our business practices. We also thought they were a result of our own inadequacies. We could not run a business, so the business had to run itself.

"Then we discovered that our approach had a serious business-school following. It is called *market-based management,* and it is studied at George Mason University. So we invited the professor to come out and explain it to us. 'Hey, that's what we already do,' said our key managers.

"It is not the only way to run a business. Nor even the best way. But it is one way."

Bonner's parting advice on leadership for CEOs is to, "Forget about leadership. Focus on the work."

4

NIRANJAN AJWANI, CEO
Ajwani Group of Companies
For me a great leader is an enabler and a facilitator.

"My style of leadership is humane," says Niranjan Ajwani of Ajwani Group. "I try to keep my leadership technique true to nature. If anything is not in harmony with nature and natural processes, it is not sustainable. I use this principle in making decisions in order to sustain happiness for myself and my teammates using our own natural strengths and rhythms to get the best out of our lives and also to sustain it.

"Leadership involves a lifelong commitment to self-mastery, to holistic living, and to a life of balance. A leader should not only harmonize his different needs, but also be an enabling and empowering factor in harmonizing the different needs of his teammates so that they enjoy work, play, love, relationships, and spiritual growth so very essential for a sustained joy.

"A great leader is an enabler and a facilitator. In actual practice we build teams with a shared vision and provide them with space, opportunity, and an environment for creativity and growth. We select members for their attitude and train them for their skills. Together we learn, we grow as a team, we create and contribute towards the progress of the enterprise—a cycle which brings workplace and personal satisfaction to each member.

"Leadership well exercised usually produces prestige, promotions, growth, customer satisfaction, business partner and associate satisfaction, stakeholder satisfaction, and win-win situations and smiles for all members of the enterprise.

"To achieve all this, a leader needs to have an integrative holistic global vision for his enterprise and has to actively promote holistic thinking and humanistic behavior within the enterprise. A good leader inspires his people with a vision of further possibilities. He works to create value for society—transcending conflict with cooperation, and transforming problems into solutions, challenges into opportunities.

"Focus is his ability to have a clear vision or goal and then moving forward to reach that goal, conscious of how the present action or activity or movement relates to it.

"We lay a lot of stress on continual education. Education within the enterprise is a lifelong process. It helps in a progressive understanding of relationships between disciplines and issues. A change in one family member of the system precipitates a change in the whole system.

"In the new millennium we have reorganized our businesses with a strong sense of purpose. The purpose of our business is to produce, offer, or deal in products and services which are useful to society and which promote the concept and practice of joyous and sustainable living, respecting nature and preserving environment. The partners we seek for our business are those who share our sense of purpose. The profits we generate out of our business are for our stockholders, who have invested in our business philosophy, products, projects, practices, and potential.

"When users of our products and services, and our partners in business and our personnel, all share our philosophy and purpose and are satisfied with our performance, business becomes a pleasure, and profits a matter of pride for us.

"The following areas have been identified within the purpose zone of our business, and revolve around the concepts of Joyous Living and Sustainable Development:

- Energy efficient, environment friendly products and services
- Educational and learning services
- House and home products
- Information Technology Services

Niranjan concludes, "I am passionate about joyous living and sustainable development."

5

DAVID T. MCLAUGHLIN, CHAIRMAN

American Red Cross

Focus on the two or three issues that will effect the future of the enterprise.

Formerly CEO of the Toro Company, David McLaughlin finds himself in a new leadership role as the nonexecutive chairman of the American Red Cross. (A nonexecutive chairman is a board chairman who does not also hold an executive position with the organization.)

"Leadership requirements of a nonexecutive chairman relate to keeping the board focused on the two or three issues that will affect the future of the enterprise, and working with management to implement the strategies that deal with these opportunities or challenges," says David.

"We did this quite successfully at the American Red Cross when after September 11, 2001, the organization had to reassess its chartered mission and to realign assets to respond to the challenges of an entirely new environment.

"The events of 9/11 changed not only the way the Red Cross prepared to respond to weapons of mass destruction disasters, but also reinforced the need to work collaboratively with other agencies that either have more capability than we do or provide needed services that are not part of our mission.

"To say that this event altered the way that the Red Cross responds to humanitarian needs and funds these efforts understates the profound changes that took place in the public's expectations of this revered organization.

"The manner in which the Red Cross responds to the 67,000 disasters we answer every year had previously been highly centralized and used technology developed some years ago. A top-level task force reassessed this system and recommended more decentralized response capacity and new technologies to make it more convenient for those affected to seek assistance. These changes are now being implemented.

The key to becoming a more effective leader, says David, "is the willingness to embrace change and to identify the opportunities that lie within that change to further the well being of the enterprise and the stakeholders of that entity."

6

A.J. WASSERSTEIN, CEO

ArchivesOne, Inc.

Never let any relationship, internal or external,
go stale or unmanaged.

When we asked A.J. Wasserstein, CEO of records management and storage company ArchivesOne, for his most important leadership secret, his immediate answer was: "Never let any relationship, internal or external, go stale or unmanaged."

Why the emphasis on relationships? It's based on the simple premise that virtually everything accomplished in the business world is done with the help of other people—especially true for managers and executives who delegate tasks to others, or workgroup members who depend on their teammates for critical information or assistance in completing their own tasks.

"You never know when you will need help or support from a person," says A.J. "If you actively manage those relationships, and keep the relationship warm, it is always easier to gain that person's cooperation."

Relationship management is not restricted to customers and employees. All relationships—potential customers, vendors, suppliers, business partners, regulatory agencies, analysts, and shareholders—require nurturing.

When asked for an example of the principle of relationship management at work, A.J. cited ArchiveOne's Alumni Acquisition Program.

"Our company is executing an acquisition program," he explains. "We have acquired eleven companies in our industry, seven in the past two years. We have an Acquisition Alumni Program where I actively communicate with the sellers of the companies we have acquired on a quarterly basis."

Often after an acquisition, the buyer and seller part company for good. But not A.J. Wasserstein. His ongoing communications with his sellers might include a handwritten note, a telephone call, mailing an interesting business book, a basket of cookies, or something related to the seller's hobbies. "We no longer have any business relationship with the sellers. We just want to maintain a nice, warm, friendly relationship."

Think this seems like a waste of a busy CEO's time? Think again. Recently, a pending acquisition candidate asked A.J. for some references to sellers whose companies he had acquired.

"This turned out to be an extremely easy request to fill, since I have warm and active relationships with all of our sellers. There were no re-introductions or favors to ask A.J. all of the sellers were delighted to assist. We got rave endorsements and won the $5.1 million deal. The deal was ours because we never let our relationships with the sellers of the companies we acquired go stale."

How can you create strong relationships with people who can help you and your business? A.J. says, "Relationships are built on a mutual exchange of explicit or implicit needs. If at minimum there is something being exchanged or provided between two parties that creates value, then a good or at least tolerable relationship can exist. If there really is nothing being exchanged that is valued by at least one party, then the relationship will probably atrophy."

Personal chemistry can help keep a weak relationship from falling apart or make an average relationship stronger. "Relationships are augmented when there is personal chemistry."

All well and good if you are a so-called people person, but what if you aren't? What if the initial chemistry between you and the other person is not strong?

"When there is a lack of chemistry, I think about why: Was there something I said or signaled that created ill will?

"The best way to identify with a person is to learn more about them by asking questions. Typically, when people learn a bit more about each other, preconceived notions are mitigated and bonding can take place.

"I hope this does not sound contrived, but I think people like other people when a genuine interest is expressed in the other person's world. Most people love telling you why they are so successful in their business, with their family, and so on. Let them brag a bit about the things that are important to them." But don't brag back. Your goal is to establish empathy, not to compete and see who's better.

"Also, a successful relationship is based on doing exactly what you say you are going to do—and a bit more. Once again, sort of simple, but it is amazing how many people just do not execute on what they promise.

"Finally, constructive relationship management thrives on ferreting out ways you can help other people with their needs to make their life easier."

Sounds sensible enough. But what do you do when a relationship has soured—for instance, when a customer is unhappy with your quality, upset about missed deliveries, or irritated by a price increase?

Wasserstein follows a simple four-step process for regaining the other party's confidence and trust in you:

1. Fully acknowledge any wrongdoing on your part.
2. Tell the other party exactly how you will set things right.
3. Fix the problem.
4. Follow up with the other party to confirm that the problem was fixed to their satisfaction.

"I know this sounds simple, and it is, but this works powerfully. It always amazes me just how forgiving people are if you acknowledge, fix, and follow up," says A.J. "When a relationship breaks down and you fix it in this fashion, you actually strengthen the relationship and create positive goodwill."

What advice does A.J. give to others who want to become better leaders?

"Leadership might be a difficult skill to learn, but a person can be a better leader by acting truly and doing the right thing in the face of adversity, when it is difficult and not the easiest choice," concludes A.J. "Observing other successful leaders and patterning your behavior characteristics on theirs can help, too."

7

CHIP PERRY, PRESIDENT AND CEO

AutoTrader.com

Challenge the status quo.

AutoTrader.com, the world's leading automotive marketplace on-line, improves the way people research, buy, and sell cars by providing a comprehensive source of information and an inventory of more than 2.2 million vehicles for sale by private sellers, dealers, and manufacturers.

As you might imagine, building a leading-edge e-business requires an innovative mindset, and AutoTrader.com CEO Chip Perry sees fostering this mindset as one of his key leadership challenges.

"My most powerful leadership technique is to tell everyone who works for AutoTrader.com that one of their main responsibilities and obligations as an employee is to constantly challenge the status quo and relentlessly work to improve whatever product, process, or system they may use to get their work done," says Chip. "Our company grew from zero to $100 million in revenues in just five years, and the main source of our success was the way our employees took the initiative to reinvent their part of the company at least once every six months.

"Most of the tools we use are created with software, which is inherently flexible and changeable. There is always room for improvement in how we help consumers shop for a car and help dealers and private owners advertise their cars for sale. It is the unending opportunity for improvement—melded with the creativity and drive of our employees—that spurs us to innovate everything we do for the benefit of our customers.

"There are so many examples of employee-driven innovation around our company that it's hard to call out just one or two. Here are a couple that stand out.

"About a year-and-a-half ago, one of our product managers came up with the idea of a *dynamic display ad* that enables car shoppers to link directly from an individual car listing to nine similar vehicles from the dealer's inventory. This *in context* shopping experience has proven very popular, since it gives consumers a way to easily see other cars they might want to buy from a dealer without doing multiple searches in our site or randomly browsing the dealer's Web site.

"This is the kind of convenience and intuitive shopping experience that the Web has the potential to deliver, but few companies are able to pull it off. More than 1,500 dealers have purchased this advertising product since it was introduced and it has become one of our best sellers.

"Incidentally, the product manager, Jeff Catron, got the idea from one of our dealer customers who thought since we already had his entire inventory online, why not let the consumer see other similar vehicles from the dealer that the consumer might want to buy?

"Another example of an employee-driven innovation is the advertising product preview tool that we recently developed so our customer service people and dealers can preview all new products before they are moved live to our Web site. This may sound like a simple idea, but it required significant new code and a set of dedicated servers. To get the project completed, it had to compete with many other priorities that are more visible on the front end of our Web site. Often it is these less visible back end improvements that are critical to employee job satisfaction, efficiency, and good customer care.

"Our culture is team-driven, so employees' support and buy-in are essential to every project's success. There are several different ways we build excitement around new ideas and initiatives.

"First, we have an internal committee called the Employee Advisory Committee. This committee is made up of individuals from each department, and their role is to provide feedback to management on new ideas. Soliciting input from our employees is the first step to gaining their support.

"Also, we plan quarterly events for our employees around new initiatives to introduce them with a bang. Depending on the department's needs, employees are trained so they have a complete understanding of the new product.

"Lastly, we have a monthly print newsletter and weekly e-newsletter that reports to our employees what is going on within the company.

Communication with our employees is key, and it definitely impacts how our employees react to new ideas and initiatives: The better we inform them, the stronger their support. Our company has been successful because of our employees' feedback and belief in our mission and goals."

How can a person learn to become a better leader? "I think a person can learn to be a better leader by remembering that the essence of management is getting things done through other people, so building the support and buy-in of the people you're working with is ultimately the most important thing managers do, and all managers who fail have somehow violated this principle.

"So many people try to be excellent individual performers, and this serves them well in their careers up to the point when they become managers. Often, as managers, they continue their habits and drive to be excellent individual performers rather than leaders that help their people get their jobs done while having fun along the way.

"Life as a manager requires people to step up and grow, and let others take credit and responsibility. That's hard to do, and that's why so many people don't make good managers or leaders.

"The best approach for individual high-performers to become effective managers is to learn from proven managers. At AutoTrader .com, we have an outstanding executive team who provides this example to our employees.

"We have a strong desire to promote from within the company, and are continuously providing professional development programs to build better managers. Our internal leadership program matches employees with a senior-level mentor. Both attend workshops and one-on-one meetings to share management experiences. This program teaches our employees that being a manager is an evolutionary process of change and growth.

"Leadership for an e-business is different than leadership for a brick and mortar. While both utilize the same fundamental leadership principles, e-businesses have a different approach in the application of these principles.

"AutoTrader.com was built from the ground up. We didn't have a detailed business plan to follow, so we adopted a *test and evolve* or *continuous improvement* mentality. We like to say, 'Nothing is written in stone.'

"Our leaders are risk takers, who are always trying to build a better mouse trap. Our company has to be more nimble, because of the ever-changing e-environment. Technology and competitors are changing all the time, and we have to move promptly and decisively. Our business has grown quickly, and we have to adapt to this growth.

"While we are a dot-com by function, we have gone beyond the start-up mode and now must evaluate ourselves differently—more like a brick and mortar—to reach the next level of success. However, this does not change who we are as a company. Setting goals and objectives now and developing a plan for the future are only making us stronger."

8

ROY VALLEE, CEO

Avnet, Inc.

*Work hard to ensure your employees are successful in
their careers and they, in turn, will work hard to
ensure your company's success.*

Like Dan Amos of AFLAC, Roy Vallee of Avnet also believes employee motivation is the key to effective leadership. "Work hard to ensure your employees are successful in their careers, and they, in turn, will work hard to ensure your company's success," Roy says.

"One of our company's strategic objectives is to develop our employees, and we invest heavily in their success. Our ten core values, which I helped establish, guide our efforts.

"Prior to 2000, we had an informal set of values, which were on a video I did for new employees. One of our groups decided to formalize them.

"Instead of allowing them to make their own list, I formed a council of our human resources, strategic planning, and corporate communications pros to help me finalize the program.

"We had a survey of employee thoughts on the issue. Then we held a few focus groups. Finally, we had a day of judgment, when we discussed and formalized the ten values. We then showed it to our executive board for final approval and announced it in November 2000. These core values are listed on our Web site at http://www.avnet.com/profile/corevalues.html.

"I announced these core values at a global general managers meeting by doing a take off of a Mel Brooks movie. Our chief lawyer played Moses holding the new values on three tablets. 'We have fifteen core values,' he announced. Then he dropped one of the tablets and said, 'We have ten core Avnet values.'

"It was a big hit and a lot of fun. We gave each manager the values on stone plaques for their office and had a variety of values merchandise they could use to market the values to all employees. Of course, we communicated the effort to all employees.

"We had a poster of the values that our top 600 managers worldwide signed in support of the values. It was printed with autographs and sent framed to all offices as a clear message of support.

"Every year, we hold a leadership conference for more than 100 executives from around the world to ensure everyone is educated about the company's goals and each other's areas of responsibility across regions and operating groups. Our Executive Development Program offers almost 30 internally developed classes. Topics include leadership, acquisitions, strategic thinking, communication skills, risk taking, and international law and finance, to name just a few, along with 'The Alchemy of a Successful Avnet Business . . . and You,' which I teach.

"As important, we are committed to providing all employees with development plans to advance their careers and offer hundreds of courses online and via a global content delivery network. Avnet offers a tuition reimbursement program as well.

"Leaders are made, not born. Keep your eyes and ears open and learn from others. Everyone has something unique to offer, and the more you listen, the better able you are to make decisions based on the broadest possible pool of information. Essentially, this means adopting a best people, best practices philosophy. When you've done your homework, you will be better equipped to make the quick, disciplined decisions that define success in today's fast-paced business world.

"Finally, become an expert in the arts of collaboration, negotiation, delegation, and communication, all of which are essential leadership skills."

Roy ended our interview with a few parting thoughts.

- Every day there are experiences that can add to an executive's development.
- It is important to know what issues to prioritize and how to deal with those issues effectively.
- Working harder is not the same as working smarter. An executive's productivity should be measured by the results, not by the hours.
- A key element to success is life balance. A person can't be at home with his family when he is working at the office.

9

DANIEL BIEDERMAN, PRESIDENT
*Bryant Park Restoration Corp./
34th Street Partnership*

*Reexamine absolutely every piece of conventional
wisdom that comes across your path.*

"By far my most powerful management and selling technique is to reexamine absolutely every piece of conventional wisdom that comes across my path. I don't believe anything until I've observed it to be true from my own experience."

Daniel Biederman is the founder of the company that designed, raised money for, received approvals for, and runs Bryant Park on a daily basis. Customers included the property-owners whose buildings abut Bryant Park, New York City, and a group of influential midtown philanthropists, led by David Rockefeller and Andrew Heiskell.

"Almost everything I have achieved was written off as unconventional, unpopular, or unlikely by someone in power, usually government. I carefully train everyone who works for me to follow me in this tendency to look skeptically at every word that is confidently pronounced by questionable authorities.

"There are some interesting subsets of this technique: don't let anyone who works for you practice law without a law degree (a common failing of 22 to 35 year olds), don't ever listen to anything told you by a building manager, and others.

"Bryant Park has dozens of examples. According to the bogus experts, movable chairs would disappear in two minutes (they never do), graffiti removed would come right back (it doesn't), privatized park management would never be accepted in New York (no one cares at all as long as it works), no good public space could ever be developed on

42nd St (as opposed to 49th St, where Rock Center is), homeless people would trash our restrooms (they haven't), and much, much more.

"A person can become a better leader by watching, working under, listening to speeches by, and reading about other leaders. It doesn't matter what field they are in, nor whether they lead men or ideas. I have learned from, among many others, Mark McCormack, Franklin D. Roosevelt, William H. Whyte, Jr., my father, Don Shula, Jim Rouse, Walt Disney, Wayne Huizinga, and Steve Wynn.

"Many business sages say that most creators and entrepreneurs aren't great managers, because the skills are thought to be different. I don't agree, and I try hard to be great at both."

10

WILLIAM H. GOODWIN, JR., CEO

CCA Industries

Make good, simple, honest, and ethical decisions.

When we asked Bill Goodwin of CCA Industries for his most powerful leadership secret, his reply was straightforward: "Make good, simple, honest, and ethical decisions."

Ah, but how do you know your decision is a good one?

"You never know whether a difficult decision is correct. In fact, you can make a difficult decision as best you can and it still could appear at a later date to not have been the right decision."

Then what do you do? "Try to get as many facts and use the best judgment you can to make the decision, and do not look back," says Bill. "The only reason you might look back is to learn something that you could have done better, so that next time you can make a better decision. The only way I know to overcome self-doubt is to be positive and learn as many facts as you can before you make a decision.

"I have tried to use this technique with all of my decisions, but the one I am most proud of was our decision to share profits from the sale of AMF Bowling with the employees. It was a good decision because it showed our employees how much we appreciated their contribution to the success of the company. It was simple because there really was no question that it was the right thing to do.

"I did not share the proceeds of the AMF sale to benefit either the company or myself, and I was looking for nothing in return. I was, however, very pleased with the gratitude that so many of the employees showed in their notes and comments after the sale."

Bill's requirement that decisions be honest stands out in a world plagued by corporate scandal. "I have never found dishonesty to be rewarding in any manner," he says. "Thus, I am always honest, regardless of the ramifications."

When asked how a person can become a better leader, he says, "Get a good education both practically and academically. Always work hard to achieve your goals, and remember to be honest and ethical."

11

JAMES M. ANDERSON, PRESIDENT

Cincinnati Children's Hospital Medical Center

Be nimble in pursuing opportunity.

"Be nimble in pursuing opportunity," is the leadership advice of hospital president James Anderson. "See opportunity, even in the face of challenges, and adjust strategy to reach goals. Be flexible, adaptive, and responsive.

"At a football game, I happened to meet and talk with an Ohio political leader. He asked why our hospital did not apply for federal funding available to hospitals for special projects.

"Until that moment, I was not aware of this funding source. Within a week, we put together a team to plan an application for funding. We selected the project and submitted a strong request within a few weeks. We received $750,000. This seeding funding helped us launch a major new surgical program for small bowel transplant."

As an academic medical center, a hospital for children, and a major research center, Cincinnati Children's Hospital Medical Center is a complex organization. Jim's leadership style is to build consensus among the various and sometimes conflicting cultures. He has created business units in which physicians, nurses, and managers work together to define and achieve shared objectives.

"The best outcome for our patients depends on teamwork among health professionals who deliver care and the multitude of others who provide the environment in which care is delivered. Our team must be able to work together for the best interest of our patients, so achieving consensus is a very good idea; it helps if we agree about our goals and methodology.

"I would say that my leadership style is to be a good listener and to seek consensus when possible. My willingness to listen and learn, and to work to achieve consensus, is not the same as abandoning the need to make decisions. I seek input from others, but ultimately as president and CEO, I make the decisions and take responsibility for them."

Jim believes good decisions are based on the facts. But is there a danger of being too reliant on data? What about trusting your gut?

"We collect and analyze data so that we are in the best possible position to make knowledgeable, informed decisions. But data is not a straight jacket. It does not control the decisions. Of course instinct plays a part, as does the recognition that we have a responsibility to the community and to the well being of children.

"For example, in recent years our community has experienced a crisis in the availability of mental health services for adolescents, because adult hospitals that had offered psychiatric services for teens closed their inpatient units due to low reimbursement rates.

"We understood the data as well as they did, but we recognized that Cincinnati Children's Hospital Medical Center has an obligation to the community. As others abandoned their responsibility, we filled the gap.

"Not only did we expand psychiatric services on our main campus, but we also purchased and renovated a facility and staffed up to open a specialized hospital for residential psychiatric care. Instinct tells me that ultimately, our stepping up to the plate to meet the community need will be in our best interest, even if business data does not support that perception."

Additional leadership advice from Jim Anderson:

- Listen. Do not jump to conclusions.
- Focus on growth and vision.
- Build a leadership team that can work together.
- Be nimble. Be ready to seize opportunities.
- Recognize mistakes early and correct them.
- When there are obstacles, look for alternative pathways to the goal.
- Never compromise organizational ethics for economic gain.

12

MATT RUBEL, CEO
Cole Haan

Ask for their best thinking and then really listen.

"My most powerful leadership technique is to ask our people for their best thinking and then really listen," says Matt Rubel, CEO of high-fashion shoemaker Cole Haan. "It shows you respect and empower those who work for you. You will come up with better answers. And those who work with you will take more pride in their own thinking and work."

Pride in work is especially important at Cole Haan, because each pair of shoes is made by a single craftsman. "He sees them all the way through the process, from beginning to end," says Matt. "And when he is satisfied that the product has been superbly executed, he puts them in the box himself—like a gift to the customer who will ultimately enjoy them.

"The best way to be a great leader is to prepare prior to meetings and interactions. Clearly articulate expectations and provide feedback mechanisms that are real and timely."

13

JOSEPH DEITCH, CEO
Commonwealth Financial Network
The primary role of the leader is to do just that—to lead.

"As trite as it may sound, the primary role of the leader is to do just that: to *lead*," says Joe Deitch of Commonwealth Financial Network. "This requires articulating a clear and powerful vision that resonates with the hearts and minds of all the people associated with the venture. While charting the right course is obviously critical, it is not enough to rally the troops and sustain their dedicated involvement.

"More specifically, the study of behavioral psychology teaches us that the most powerful motivators share certain characteristics. They are (1) positive, (2) reliable, and (3) immediate. Thus while a negative motivator such as fear may promote some baseline behaviors, it certainly won't motivate people to go above and beyond for an extended time.

"As for reliability, it stands to reason that the higher our chance of being rewarded, be it tangible or psychological satisfaction, the more we will take a goal seriously. Likewise, the immediate reward is much more enticing and reinforcing than some vague promise, which may or may not materialize in the distant future.

"Putting it all together, the art of effective leadership requires coordinating the needs and desires of the individual with the direction of the company. Goals must be important and worthy if they are to be embraced. People will move mountains to protect cherished values and/or to significantly advance their own lot in life. Conversely, few will get excited about improving meaningless measurements. Goals must have meaning!

"For example, in 2001, Commonwealth chose a significant service initiative as its primary campaign. Then, in 2002, our major campaign was to dramatically improve efficiency and profitability, while never losing sight of service.

"The approach to each campaign was consistent. We are a service company, and therefore we are only as good as the service we provide. This is how we measure our success, both individually and corporately.

"At the start of 2001, senior management decided that we were ready to raise the service bar well above our competitors. We wanted to deliver a level of service that was so remarkable that our customers would consider us to be *indispensable.*

"The first step was to take this idea to all of our managers and then to all of our employees. We were looking at first for consensus and buy-in. We didn't want to be moving the company in a direction where our people did not want to go; rather we wanted everyone to be enthusiastically pushing in the same direction.

"The new goal resonated deeply with one and all. Most people, or at least the ones we want on our team, very much want to take pride in their work and be better than the competition. Furthermore, this ties directly into the growth, stability and profitability of the firm. Everyone was on board.

"The next steps involved creating teams to brainstorm, develop subsidiary programs, and coordinate the various people, departments, and technologies that we utilize. The achievement of goals and the associated rewards cannot be left to chance. The company must develop specific systems to track progress, make adjustments where necessary, keep everyone informed and interested, celebrate every success, and continuously reinforce what we were doing and why.

"Just as a movie is choreographed to maintain our interest and provide increasing payback to the audience, so must a company and its leadership create the systems to motivate everyone involved in the project throughout the entire journey. And that is exactly what we did. Since the start of the campaign, our average annual Service Scores provided by representatives have risen from 85 percent to 92 percent.

"As for profitability, when the economy fizzled in 2000 and 2001, it left many companies with inflated payrolls and inefficient operations. The economic growth had been so rapid that we had been much more focused on keeping up with demand than fine-tuning operations.

But all that had changed, and in 2002 it was time to focus on fiscal management.

"While cutting costs may not be as much fun as raising service to new heights, we all had a huge vested interest in keeping Commonwealth financially strong. Not only does the firm provide our weekly paycheck, it also serves as an important community where we spend more time than any other place in our lives.

"Realizing the significant nature of our undertaking, meetings were held to flesh out the new campaign. In doing so, we realized that it was important to articulate the fact that while healthy net margins are critical, we would put equal weight on maintaining our legendary service levels. Indispensable service was here to stay. Once again, committees were chosen, tasks were assigned, goals were created, everything was measured, and everyone was kept informed.

"Knowing in advance that this would be difficult, the initial campaign was presented as a manageable three-month process. During this time, much progress was made and successes were acknowledged.

"Ultimately however, there were two more phases. The second focused on cross-pollinating the various ideas and successes developed in all of the individual departments. This was also promoted as a huge opportunity for managerial learning and development.

"The third and final phase had the biggest focus on rewards. Contests were announced in a myriad of categories, and consciously designed with an opportunity for virtually every one and every department to receive recognition for their success in one of the three phases.

"When it was all over, there was a great celebration where we acknowledged everyone's individual achievements.

"Any campaign of this nature is stressful and I wanted to provide our people with positive feelings and memories. The camaraderie was extremely satisfying. In addition to the beautiful globe that everyone received to commemorate our success, we also gave everyone a significant cash bonus—instead of handing out a few prizes, we decided to acknowledge that this was indeed a team effort by a great team, and we would all share equally.

"While it's great to read books and learn from others, ultimately we need to look within. No plan will succeed if it is at odds with our inner self. Rather than trying to justify something we don't truly believe in, it's so much better to leverage our core beliefs and our personal passions.

"The clearer we are about our own desires, the better able we are to articulate a noble cause to others. Our passion can speak directly to their passion. It's real and it's much more powerful than any speech we could concoct.

"We also live in a world with an infinite number of competing distractions. Any campaign worth leading requires conscious execution. Messages must be repeated and reinforced—and delivered in the moral language of the intended audience. Rewards must be targeted to the individual recipients to be meaningful. Progress must be tracked and communicated so that everyone knows that this is important, this is real, and that they are making an important contribution.

"The leader chooses the course, drives the bus, and keeps his or her eyes, ears, and heart open. For the conscious leader, every act is an opportunity to learn—and improve. In doing so, the journey continues and the experience becomes richer for all concerned."

14

SANJAY KUMAR, CHAIRMAN AND CEO

Computer Associates International, Inc.

A leader must be able to make change happen.

"The IT industry is rife with 'visions,' but too often fails to deliver on its pronouncements," says Sanjay Kumar of Computer Associates. "It's not enough to recognize the need for change. A leader must be able to make it happen, by guiding an organization through the process and driving transformation throughout a company's culture. To do that quickly and effectively, a leader must have both the ability to build consensus and the willingness to decide actions when necessary.

"Computer Associates has succeeded as a cutting-edge technology company because of its ability to change—time and again—to meet the demands of a dynamic business. We owe our agility to the exceptional quality of our people, who are quick to recognize challenges and opportunities, and coalesce around a strategy for success.

"Moreover, because they are engaged in producing innovative enterprise software that solves real business problems, our people have intimate knowledge of our customers' evolving needs, which inspires them to become agents for change in their own right.

"In leading the most talented software developers, product managers, and business unit executives in the IT industry, my job is to encourage individual initiative and the 'creative cacophony' that produces innovation, while ensuring that we work toward common goals and objectives. It's a balancing act predicated on a consensus that the customer must be at the center of everything we do.

"Back in 2000, just before the really large potholes started to appear in the IT landscape, we decided that a change in course was necessary. We completely transformed our business model, a decision that incurred considerable risk and generated significant controversy. We reworked everything in order to give our customers a simpler, more flexible, and more cost-effective way to use and license our software.

"With our FlexSelect model, we let them decide how much, for how long, and on what basis they would like to license our products. Under this new approach, we've strived to reduce the term of contracts from an average length of five to six years in 2000, to three years or less today. Customers like this change because history has taught them a lot about how rapidly software technology changes. They appreciate the flexibility to move on, without penalty, to something more suited to their needs after only a couple of years.

"FlexSelect also helps eliminate the wrenching end-of-quarter purchase and discounting decisions that characterize much of the unproductive give and take between vendors and customers in the software business.

"The flexibility of FlexSelect even extends to how we get paid. For instance, a mobile phone company that licenses our software to manage its infrastructure pays us based on the number of subscribers. A European airline pays us based on passenger kilometers flown.

"In each case, payment is based on a metric that measures business success. Our FlexSelect licensing enables us to tailor our solutions to our customers' needs.

"At its core, the new FlexSelect business model moves away from a traditional method of recording almost all of our license revenue upfront, to a method that records license revenue over the term of the agreement. Instituting this model required our people to completely rethink the way Computer Associates—indeed, every company in our industry—had been doing business for decades.

"Changing the traditional software licensing model required an intensive internal consensus-building effort around the idea that our company's future would depend on the quality of our relationships with customers as much as it does on the quality of our technology. That was the easy part, because our own people had little difficulty in recognizing economic forces that demanded such a shift—and the benefits it would generate for our customers and our company. However, I would say that we underestimated how much difficulty some members of the investment community would have in understanding the rationale behind the move.

"That said, three years later, we are proud of the fact that our business model has given us a significant competitive advantage, particularly in today's challenging economic environment. What's more, we are starting to see other large software companies move toward our model.

"I believe to a large extent becoming a good leader starts with surrounding yourself with people who are smarter than you. We try to teach our management team that they can't and shouldn't do everything themselves—that is, gathering all required information, performing all of the detailed analysis, and making all the decisions. Leaders must be able to delegate and rely on the good people supporting them, and they must learn to trust others. Leaders also must be extremely good listeners.

"But when it comes time to make a decision, leaders must step up and make a judgment given the best input they have. And then it's time to move on to the next item on the agenda."

15

ARCHIE W. DUNHAM, CHAIRMAN

ConocoPhillips

*Focus. You cannot go everywhere and do
everything if you expect to perform well.*

"I learned a powerful leadership secret when I was in the United
States Marine Corps. It was called the Five Ps: Prior planning prevents
poor performance.

"Whether in the military or in business, preparation is critical," says
Archie Dunham. "One reason why the Marines are so successful is the
thoroughness with which they plan; they evaluate alternatives, they anticipate what can go wrong, and they provide for contingencies.

"When I participated in maneuvers as a young lieutenant, I kept a
notebook where I logged every mistake and each area where we could
improve. Then I shared the benefits of this ongoing education with the
young lieutenants who followed me.

"I did the same thing in the business world as I rose in the corporate ranks and had the opportunity to train our young, high-potential
managers. Consequently, for the rest of my career, I almost never went
to a meeting unprepared. Equally important, I had a management team
behind me that was trained to think and act the same way.

"Prior planning always pays off—and never more so than when the
time came to realize my long-time dream to make Conoco an independent company again. Conoco had merged with DuPont in 1981 to avoid
a hostile takeover. By 1998, the original justification for the merger had
evaporated, and there were compelling reasons for us to break free of
DuPont.

"But regaining independence was a massive undertaking that required meticulous planning. That we succeeded in realizing the objective was due entirely to our attention to detail.

"We had to marshal compelling arguments to persuade DuPont's board that it was in the shareholders' best interest for us to separate. That meant extensive in-house planning and research.

"We didn't trust our own brainpower alone. We brought in outside investment bankers and financial experts—first, to help us make the case to our board, and then to lay the groundwork for the initial public offering (IPO). We also hired our own legal counsel to help us negotiate our way through the transition, rather than relying on DuPont's legal department. Extensive planning pervaded every step in the process.

"In the end, the planning was rewarded even beyond our fondest expectations. When the Conoco stock began trading on the floor of the New York Stock Exchange on October 22, 1998, the IPO was greatly oversubscribed. In fact, at $4.4 billion, it was the largest IPO in U.S. history up to that time.

"The first quality of effective leadership is focus. You cannot go everywhere and do everything if you expect to perform well. You have to focus your attention on your most important priorities each day.

"Being effective doesn't depend on how much effort you expend or how many hours you work. Being effective means focusing on what really matters.

"Successful leaders concentrate on their most important priorities. Most failures are caused by a lack of focus."

16

WILLIAM G. CRUTCHFIELD, JR., CEO

Crutchfield Corp.

The fundamental role of a successful leader is to achieve alignment.

Crutchfield's CEO, Bill Crutchfield, feels that the fundamental role of a successful leader is to achieve alignment. "Much is written about executives' roles in aligning their teams around corporate strategy and tactics," he says. "Kenneth Lay was probably very effective in this capacity at Enron.

"Unfortunately, too little is written or taught about the alignment of values and the creation of strong organizational cultures. The most powerful leadership technique that I know is identifying, inculcating, and managing an organizational culture.

"Leaders must possess the right set of core values and must be able to align everyone in their organizations around those values. Obviously, if Mr. Lay had possessed the right values, and created a healthy organizational culture and aligned his employees around them, Enron would not have collapsed in scandal."

But what values should a leader embrace? "In a capitalistic society, there is always the temptation to do what it takes to get rich quickly. Aligning a company around those values too often leads to serious problems," says Bill. "From my experience, I find that truly successful leaders possess values that are centered on responsibly serving the best interests of customers, employees, business partners and stakeholders over the long run.

"Another tough issue is how one balances the best interests of these various constituents. It is a very difficult balancing act. If you 'give away the store' to delight your customers, you obviously are not acting in the best interest of the stakeholders.

"On the other hand, if you are not genuinely sensitive to your customers' needs, you will never gain their loyalty. If you view your employees and business partners as overhead that needs to be minimized for the benefit of the stakeholders, you may miss a great opportunity.

"When treated with respect, and when the appropriate human and financial resources are invested, they become tremendous assets to an organization. And, if you concentrate too much on maximizing the wealth of senior management, you can ruin the business. The financial mania of the late 1990s lured many executives into making self-serving decisions that ended up hurting all of their constituents—customers, employees, business partners, and, ironically, themselves."

How can one align people around ones' values? Bill says, "The obvious first step is to live them fully. A leader must be the embodiment of the organization's core values.

"The next step is to communicate those values constantly. A leader must be an evangelist for inculcating the organization's core values. Then, you must ensure that the organization has management systems that maintain these values.

"Crutchfield is a consumer electronics company. We sell primarily through mail order catalogs and online, and we also have two stores.

"We hire people based on our assessment of their ability to adapt to our core values. We include compliance with our basic beliefs into our employee reviews. And, we reward and discipline our people based on their compliance.

"When a leader does all of this, his or her business will have the best possible competitive advantage—a powerful institutional culture built around the long-term needs of customers, employees, business partners, and stakeholders. To me, the successful accomplishment of this objective is an excellent demonstration of leadership. Unfortunately, it is not an element of leadership that is widely understood or frequently addressed.

"Our sales continued to grow each year through 1982. However, the rate of growth kept slowing. Even more disturbing, our earnings started to erode considerably. We placed the blame on the recession and assumed our fortunes would improve when the national economy did.

"In 1983, the economy did rebound vigorously. However, our sales fell by 10 percent and earnings turned negative. Our cash dwindled rapidly as a result of these losses and the construction costs of a new building. By spring, I had to take out a bank loan.

"The losses continued to grow, and by late summer the loan had grown considerably. Although the company still had a substantial net worth, these losses deeply concerned me, my executives and, of course, the bankers. Something was fundamentally wrong with the company.

"In searching for the answer, I received mixed input. One of our vice presidents championed the argument that our strategy was wrong. He and his supporters strongly believed that we were adding too much value to our products and, therefore, had to charge higher prices than our mail order competitors.

"They recommended that we adopt the strategy of a mail order company in Baltimore. Their catalog was crude in comparison to ours. It had no helpful articles, was printed on newsprint, and used line drawings of products instead of photographs. This company did not offer the services that we provided our customers: toll-free sales, customer service and technical assistance lines, installation guides, liberal return privileges, technical services department, or repair shop.

"However, their prices were lower than ours and they were reported to be very successful. My staff's strong recommendation was that we strip our business down and compete head-to-head with this company. I was so convinced that the stripped-down catalog approach would have been a disaster that I made a 'command' decision not to follow their advice.

"A totally different recommendation came from the University of Virginia's McIntire School of Commerce. Crutchfield Corporation was selected for the 1984 McIntire Commerce Invitational case. The faculty case writer conducted most of his interviews with me during the fall of 1983 when I was searching for the solution. He wrote in the case, 'Crutchfield Corporation has gotten bigger than Bill Crutchfield can handle.' From this, I assumed his recommendation was that I should be replaced as my company's CEO.

"Fortunately, I did not follow his recommendation either. Instead, I spent a great deal of time thinking about the problem philosophically. Rather than analyzing how the numbers had changed over the years, I thought of how the soul of the company had changed.

"When the business was much smaller, it embodied my beliefs—caring for customers, respecting employees, working closely with our business partners, and striving for perfection. However, what I saw now in the company was a culture out of phase with my beliefs.

"The salespeople cared more about their commission checks than about the welfare of our customers. Our warehouse had become so bureaucratic that it was taking several days to ship an order instead of

24 hours. Our customer service people viewed their role more to protect management from angry customers than to find solutions to our customers' problems.

"I realized that employees were not respecting each other to the degree that they once had. Morale was bad, turnover was high and cooperation was poor.

"Finally, I realized that we no longer tried to be at the leading edge of everything we did. The design of the catalogs had slipped. The product copy lacked excitement. Our catalog merchandising was confused. Packages weren't well packed. Our sales and technical advisors were inadequately trained. Our store was not neat or well merchandised. Basically, the culture of the company had slowly and insidiously evolved into something very different than what it had been only a few years before.

"During this intellectual probing, I read a statement that was so appropriate to our situation that it was almost uncanny. Thomas Watson, Jr., made it during a lecture at Columbia University in 1962. The IBM Chairman said, 'I firmly believe that any organization, in order to survive and achieve success, must have a sound set of beliefs on which it premises all its policies and actions. Next, I believe that the most important factor in corporate success is faithful adherence to those beliefs. And, finally, I believe that if an organization is to meet the challenges of a changing world, it must be prepared to change everything about itself except those beliefs as it moves through corporate life.'

"Now I understood exactly what the problem was. The company did have a set of beliefs—my beliefs. While the company was small, I was instinctively able to ensure that everyone adhered to them. As it grew, I lost this control, and my beliefs and the company's beliefs gradually started to diverge. By 1983, they were very different. Since this change had occurred so slowly, I never recognized the problem until I read Mr. Watson's comments.

"Once you discover a problem, the answer is relatively easy. Initially, I defined and wrote three basic beliefs. Soon I added the fourth. Over the past twenty years, the wording has evolved into the following:

1. Exceed our customers' expectations by providing a truly exceptional level of integrity, courtesy, service, and helpful information.
2. Maintain a passion for continuous improvement through commitments to excellence, productive change and innovation.
3. Respect each of our coworkers and provide a work environment that promotes dignity, team harmony, and personal satisfaction.

4. Respect our business partners and maintain mutually rewarding relationships with vendors who demonstrate high professional standards.

"Next, I had to articulate them to everyone in the company. The beliefs were attractively printed and given to each employee. In group meetings, I briefed everyone on exactly what they meant and how our employees were expected to adhere to them. Finally, I created the systems that inculcated them into our company's culture and ensured their adherence.

"I made the first item on our employee review form, 'Adherence to our Basic Beliefs.' Top management then started an extensive review process. Depending on how they complied with the basic beliefs, employees were retained in their current positions, promoted, demoted and, in a few cases, terminated. Very quickly, everyone got the message.

"Almost overnight, the company started to change. Employees cared more about our customers. They worked much more closely with their fellow employees. They gained respect for our business partners. And, they started to show a genuine commitment to excellence in the performance of their jobs.

"Sales started to grow again. The company quickly returned to profitability. Within a year, we were achieving results that exceeded our wildest expectations.

"On the other hand, I am confident that the company would have failed if I had not identified the problem and led a cultural revolution to correct it.

"As for the competitor my vice president had wanted me to emulate, they filed for bankruptcy."

17

S. MICHAEL JOSEPH, CEO
DACOR Distinctive Appliances
Orient your company to a higher purpose.

"What is my most powerful leadership secret? To orient my company to a higher purpose and to be consistent in following our moral compass," says Mike Joseph, CEO of DACOR, a high-end kitchen appliance manufacturer.

"I've been with DACOR 32 years. During this period, sales have increased from $50,000 to approaching $200,000,000. The company has nearly doubled in size since the inception of the DACOR Value Statement five years ago."

A recent project: conducting a Value Training workshop with his executive team. The Value Statement reads:

To Honor God in All That We Do . . .

- By respecting others
- By doing good work
- By helping others
- By forgiving others
- By giving thanks
- By celebrating our lives

"I believe that when we respect and help one another, we are able to recognize the talent throughout the organization. When we practice forgiveness and give thanks to one another, we open and improve communication. When we deliver innovative and high-quality products, we do good work. When our business behavior is driven by these values, everyone benefits, and we have many reasons to celebrate our lives.

"Also, we began to understand that in a company that truly manages by its values, there is only one boss—the company values.

"In the context of the rest of the world, bringing spiritual values into the daily workplace is considered a bold step. If other leaders face the challenge I did—that is, wondering if I should go forward with acknowledging God's presence at work—my advice is absolutely go ahead and do it!

"Now, my entire executive team and I have participated in the Values Training Workshops; they have trained their staff, and so on. Our goal is to have every DACOR associate participate in these small group-training sessions in the next few months. It will be an ongoing process as we are challenged daily in the workplace to make value based decisions.

"Five years ago, when I developed the internal initiative to change the way we approach business, I wanted an inclusive statement, and a call to a higher purpose. One encounters cynicism when one begins to implement a Value Statement.

"First, we presented to employee groups and distributor groups. Some individuals were uncomfortable. Nevertheless, I simply wanted to find the right words to express the moral compass for the company. And words are important, though actions are more important. Now, we communicate the company Value Statement everywhere: Web, business cards, and showrooms. People have embraced it internally and externally.

"There are many tangible examples of how we put the Value Statement into action.

- Profits are shared with our associates.
- Each associate is a stockholder through our Employee Stock Ownership Program.
- Our products are innovative—many industry firsts to our credit.
- Our product warranty is most generous in industry.
- We have a proactive customer service department.
- We have a free employee assistance program: a 24 hour help hotline.
- Each new associate is personally welcomed by me.
- Each associate receives a birthday card from me each year (a small gesture, but significant).

- We say Grace at our associate luncheons and close with a benediction.
- The Value Statement is shown on the Web page, business cards, offices, and showrooms.
- We strive for consistent communication through such things as our *OnValue* newsletter.
- Charitable work is encouraged through our community outreach department.

"On the personal side, my wife Lynn and I founded the Joseph Family Foundation, dedicated to helping children live healthy, fulfilling, spiritual lives, and to strengthening the bonds of family.

"Gratefully, our associates demonstrate their support of what we do in many ways:

- Less than 10 percent attrition rate
- 96.6 percent acceptance of the Value Statement in a recent anonymous survey
- High productivity—our sales per employee is 77 percent higher than the industry median
- Operating income per employee and market value per employee among the highest in the industry

"Introducing the Value Statement has truly had a transformative effect throughout the company, and it has taken everyone to make it work. I'm the guy who was inspired to take the first step. Now, it is very gratifying to see how the company now 'owns' it."

Mike's advice for becoming a better leader is to, "create an environment where your employees can do their best work. If you do, they will do extraordinary things. Also, one must have a mindset that he is primarily responsible for the welfare of the people he leads. As I was taught in the Marine Corps: An officer eats after his men are fed.

"Other ways to become a better leader are to:

- Understand that education is a continuous process—be open to new ideas.
- Have a willingness to show your humanity.
- Exhibit and engender trust—trust God, trust yourself, and trust others.
- Encourage people to take risks.
- Be consistent with the journey you are on.

"To be a better leader, one must be the kind of person others can trust. That means, consistency, humility, integrity. It means unfailing honesty with people. Treat them as what they are—creations of God.

"For example, I make it a point to spend some time with every person who joins the company. These are folks who work 8 hours a day at DACOR, yet they also spend 16 hours of their lives as mothers, fathers, sisters, and/or brothers. They face challenges of life outside DACOR. To be better leaders, we need to respect the people that we are privileged to lead. It is the principle of servant leadership.

"I also believe it is important to decide to develop a different kind of company, connect with people on a different level, and be perceived as a different company in the marketplace and by your employees."

18

TERDEMA USSERY, PRESIDENT AND CEO

Dallas Mavericks

Have a vision and translate that vision to everybody in the organization with passion and conviction.

"The key to leadership is to have a vision and translate that vision to everybody in the organization with passion and conviction," says Dallas Mavericks CEO Terdema Ussery.

When he was appointed CEO of the team in 1997, he quickly announced his vision to make the Dallas Mavericks "the best sports entertainment company in the country."

With the emphasis on entertainment, the most important measurement of success is fan satisfaction—did the fan have a great experience watching the game?

One of his innovative ideas for soliciting customer feedback was to put his personal e-mail address up on the scoreboard at home games. Fans were told, "If you send an e-mail, we will get back to you personally by the end of that day. If we don't, then don't support us."

Says Terdema, "One fan sent an e-mail in the first quarter saying he couldn't find the game on TV. I called our broadcast partner, and together we called the fan at home within ten minutes of receiving his e-mail. We then showed him how to get the game on his TV. He could not believe that we had called him personally."

Another improvement came from fan feedback when attendees at home games complained that seats in the upper level were too far away to hear the game. "The solution was to mike the rims and floor so people in the upper level could hear every slam dunk and sneaker squeak."

Also, when people in the upper level complained they could not see the 24-second clock, Terdema bought and had installed a new three-sided clock to accommodate them.

"Eleven thousand people sit in the upper levels," he explains. "The cost of these improvements was minimal, but the impact phenomenal.

"Only your customers can tell you whether you are doing things wrong or right. We listen to them through our e-mail, through which we get comments every day.

"It used to be in the business world that companies didn't listen. We keep our ear to the ground, hear what people are telling us, and adjust and adapt based on this feedback."

The results speak for themselves: The Mavericks played to a sell-out crowd in 71 consecutive home games. In addition, in surveys from ESPN and JD Powers, the Mavericks consistently garner top ratings from fans.

19

SALVADOR DIAZ-VERSON, JR., PRESIDENT

Diaz-Verson Capital Investments, LLC (DVC)

Conduct your business with honorable intentions.

"The most fundamental leadership secret that comes to mind is the value of personal honor. When you conduct business with honorable intentions and you respond to your peers, employees, and customers with an attitude of honesty and fairness, they generally respond in kind.

Salvador Diaz-Verson of investment firm DVC believes that a leader must develop a vision for the organization. "A vision is a mind snapshot of what the organization could be. The vision must be in clear focus and detailed, in full living color. It must be desired beyond any mere goal or want a person otherwise possesses.

"It must be so vivid to the holder (visionary), so clearly desirable, that the holder can describe it with such passion that others nearly immediately catch the contagion. It must be of such import to the holder that sacrifices can be endured, and setbacks do not deter him from his path. It is not obsession, but it's very, very close.

"The most common mistake I see is that people tend to confuse a mere want with a true vision. Just because you want to be a leader, or want to run a Fortune 500 company, or want to be wealthy, does not mean you have a vision.

"Usually, wealth is a byproduct, not a part of the vision itself. You develop a vision by connecting the dots of what is to form a picture of what could be. You examine the vision, fine-tune it, and fill in the holes. Then, you figure out how to get there, usually with the help of other people.

"That does not mean taking a soft approach to business opportunities or problem resolutions. Honor is not a weakness; it is strength. Simply put, say what you mean and do what you say every time.

"In the way of leadership technique, my first order of business is to eradicate encapsulated thought patterns and trendy reactions. An *encapsulated thought pattern* is an oversimplified thought or answer to a very broad problem or condition packaged in a single word or phrase that triggers a set response.

"Think Pavlov's dog—bell rings, dog salivates, even when food is not present. Bell equals hunger. In the case of business, overused words and phrases produce a similar automatic response.

"For example: *think outside the box* means 'discard tried-and-true methods, eliminate experience in favor of new approaches.' The phrase was not originally intended to be so interpreted; yet that is the effect.

"Business cannot rely on clichés—old encapsulated thought patterns—or trendy catchphrases, which are nothing more than new encapsulated thought patterns. So, encapsulated thought patterns exclude options that could be crucial to really solving a problem or seizing an opportunity. Any word or phrase that discounts youth, age, technology, experience, focus, or any another variable compromises the equation and disables the function of reasoning.

"Critical thinking skills using facts and logic are essential to our success and to any business, really, but logical thought processes can easily be eroded or undermined by trends and even buzzwords. Catchy phrases like *think outside the box* form an encapsulated thought pattern that can stifle critical thinking and diminish productivity.

"In our company, an employee is given a job title and a list of specific responsibilities, because that is precisely the function I want that person to perform, and which I will hold him or her accountable for. That job is 'the box,' and I want that person focusing on the box's content—the responsibilities and the goals therein, including working within the scope of the bigger picture and in tandem with the other boxes.

"Thinking 'inside the box' is not an isolated exercise but a good, clear, clean focus on the job at hand. So, I do not want people thinking outside the box. I want them thinking outside of the ordinary.

"Once an employee understands this concept, something everyone is introduced to from day one, I give that person sufficient control and authority to match the level of responsibility of that position or job, and then I step back and let him or her do their thing.

"I expect the top management people in any of my ventures to initiate action and dialogue with me. I do not micromanage, and I don't want my people waiting around for marching orders. I expect them to think outside of the ordinary and thus deliver extraordinary results.

"In this world, there are leaders and tyrants. If a person merely wants to order people around, he or she is a tyrant. No learning is necessary, since callous abuse of others is a rudimentary, primal brain function. Any moron can do it—and most will, if ever given the chance.

"If, however, a person wishes to become a leader or a better leader, then the process begins by examining one's own skill strengths, moral code, people skills, and big-picture abilities. You don't become a better leader by changing other people; you become a better leader by improving yourself.

"This is not about rounding up the herd. It's about developing yourself into something other people want to follow naturally. If people follow you because they believe in you, because you offer a vision and a reach they aspire to, because they can trust both your ability and your word, then you will foster loyalty among your followers.

"Loyalty among the ranks is crucial to great leadership. The higher the career ladder you climb, the larger the number of underlings, and the greater your vulnerability to both sabotage and protection from individuals in that crowd. Lead well or fall badly.

"A tyrant can drive a company to be extremely profitable. However, his life is usually in tatters. Paranoid, miserable, lonely tyrants often have nothing outside of material wealth. They usually live to rue the day they set foot on that path. Castro is afraid to sleep at night, and Saddam dares not show his face. A similar fate often awaits tyrants in business. And dying lonely, miserable, and universally hated is not my definition of success."

20

MARK DIMASSIMO, CEO
DiMassimo Brand Advertising

Ask questions.

Mark DiMassimo says that his most powerful leadership secret or technique is asking questions.

"In the ten years I worked for other agencies, before starting DiMassimo Brand Advertising in 1996, I knew that my goal was to one day found a truly great agency. I considered every job I had continuing education, so I never hesitated to hire people who were older, better, and much more highly paid than I was.

"The most important question I asked every single one of them was, 'What was the best place you ever worked?' I'd follow up with, 'What made it the best place to work?' These discussions could go on for hours because I never tired of the subject, and I found that even for the best people, a great work experience is rare—they loved talking about it too.

"The common theme was *competence*. 'We were just good at what we did.' That's the representative quote.

"Of course, I learned so much more from those conversations that I put into use every day, but I never forget how crucial and how rare competence is. This helps me make the tough decisions I might otherwise put off. Every day.

"People often comment on the quality of the people at our agency. And people who are new to the agency often remark on the quality of our clients, both as people and as marketers, and of the partners and vendors we work with. This is not a coincidence. Great people attract great people.

"Before anyone gets hired by DiMassimo Brand Advertising, they must be interviewed by me. I don't rush. Sometimes the interview can take two hours; sometimes it takes more than one interview.

"I have a little test I do with every single applicant. It is simply the most effective question I've found for understanding a potential team member: What gives you satisfaction?

"I hand them a piece of paper and a pencil and I ask them to make a list of ten things they've done in their lives that they remember with satisfaction. I tell them that this shouldn't include 'interview answers.' That 'I broke up with my boyfriend' could be an excellent answer.

"One inflexible rule is that five of the answers must come from before their 18th birthday. These early successes tell a lot.

"For me it was the short story I wrote in the seventh grade, and the effect it had on my parents and the head of the English department at my school. The feeling of power!

"I study these lists, both with the prospective team member and after the interview. I look for themes, like courage, creativity, independence, adventure, rebellion, belonging, discovery. Once I have a sense of a candidate, I can match the satisfaction to the job. This helps not only with hiring, but with every interaction with that team member for as long as we work together. I feel I have a sense from the beginning how things will go right and how things could go wrong with this person. It's a good question.

"How can a person learn to become a better leader?" asks Mark. "The best way is to work for a good leader, in the sort of context you want to be a better leader in. Leadership is contextual. In my industry, the great leader of a global agency isn't very much like the great leader of an independent creative agency. They are both highly competent, but the competence is distinct.

"Then learn by asking ever better questions. There are shallow people who can be successful for a time, but sooner or later they find themselves in unfamiliar territory and the good times end.

"Through questions you become sophisticated, you see distinctions other don't, and you identify danger where others miss it and opportunity as well. You solve problems other fail to see.

"Most people would rather talk than listen, but the payoff on listening is immense."

21

HURLEY CALISTER TURNER, JR., CHAIRMAN
Dollar General Corporation

Leadership is the art of human relations.

"To me, there is no leadership secret, nor does effective leadership conform to 'technique,'" says Cal Turner, chairman of retail giant Dollar General. "To the extent leadership secrets exist at all, they are available in the most widely published but least read of all books: The Holy Bible."

What does the Bible have to do with business leadership? Says Cal, "Leadership is the art of human relations. The fundamentals of the art, the dynamics of relationships, are right there in the good book.

"Mature self-knowledge is the prerequisite of effective leadership. A God-centered discovery of self is one's best determination of the *what* of leadership (mission, purpose, and intended results) and also the *how* of eliciting followership from other flawed human beings. It is 'psychological' (spiritual) maturity, which prompts the leadership mandate and the followership response.

"The Bible is all about being grounded in solid values and a long-term mission that matters. So is leadership, whose true test is consistent long-term accomplishment. While communication is the highest skill of a leader, even effective communication that is short term or manipulative is the mere personality projection of a nonleader.

"My best lessons have been my failures. Every leader knows that the best insights are out there where the problems occur. Problem solving genius resides in the common sense of the persons with firsthand experience of the problem. Yet gleaning that wisdom has been my greatest challenge in management. How many of my failures do you have time to consider? Three actual examples now come to mind.

"First, hourly paid store employees at Dollar General have proven to be better merchants than company merchants not in daily relationship with our customers. Our merchants once decided to get a bigger sale from our popular three for $1 microwave popcorn. They tried an eight for $2 package (greater value than three for $1—right?) The resulting fall-off in sales had them baffled. But a store employee explained, 'Mr. Turner, our customers can only spend a dollar at a time on popcorn.' That insight got our business popping again, thanks to the new package of four for $1.00—great value at the right price point.

"But a retailer's real strategic marketing geniuses are her customers. Oh, for the skill of truly getting what the customer is saying! Here are two of my mistakes. The first involves not understanding the customer's lingo or terminology.

"An African-American customer who regularly shopped us and our major competitor once told me our prices were lower in every category except health and beauty aids. Back to our merchants I went to survey pricing on toothpaste, deodorant, shampoo, and aspirin. Our prices were all lower. I decided the customer was mistaken.

"However, a couple of years later I learned that our prices on ethnic hair care products were higher because they were distributed by a third party, while the competition directly distributed these health and beauty aids. My failure to clarify the customer's definition delayed great category sales by two years.

"My second mistake involves aggressive ego-centered communication for a misunderstood customer message. Touring one of our stores with the manager, I tried to help an elderly lady who was disappointed by our Advil out-of-stock. Convinced that our house brand Ibuprofen (with *my* signature on the bottle guaranteeing satisfaction) was just what she needed, I applied my best CEO salesmanship. She refused adamantly because she did not like the color. Well, I told her, 'I could change the color for you, maybe!'

"'Young man,' she said blushing, 'you definitely cannot change the color even if your signature *is* on the bottle. After I leave the store, let your manager tell you what I mean.'

"Later the manager told me he knew I would fail to make the sale because that lady was convinced that our Ibuprofen *turns her urine a funny color.*"

Cal's final piece of advice for being a better leader: "Listen to your followers. What are they really saying? What are they leaving *unsaid?*"

22

DAVID A. BRANDON, CHAIRMAN AND CEO
Domino's Pizza

Listen to the people who are closest to the customers and the marketplace. They will give you your best advice and input.

"There are no leadership secrets that I am aware of!" says David Brandon, CEO of Domino's Pizza. "My experience tells me that it is important to be a coach and a teacher. Lead by example. Articulate a vision. Find out how people want to be treated and treat them that way. Build a great team. Surround yourself with people smarter than you are.

"Study effective leaders. Read what they write. Listen to them speak. Observe what effective leaders do right and emulate them. Observe what lousy leaders do wrong and avoid their mistakes.

"Don't be afraid to admit that you don't always have all the answers. Just because you are made the leader of an organization doesn't mean you suddenly possess all knowledge and experience on every facet of the enterprise. Listen to the people who are closest to the customers and the marketplace. They will give you your best advice and input.

"Don't be afraid to ask for help. You will need a lot of it if you plan to be a successful leader.

"If you want to know whether someone is a good leader, ask the people who work for them. They will tell you what is real."

Domino's vision statement reads, "Exceptional people on a mission to be the best pizza delivery company in the world." As part of this vision, David has a list of goals he wants to achieve.

- Opening the 10,000th Domino's store worldwide
- Being named one of the 100 best companies to work for in America

- Becoming a Fortune 500 company that regularly exceeds the expectations of its investors
- Continuing to grow market share in the pizza delivery category worldwide
- Becoming known as the employer of choice among all quick-service restaurant companies
- Attaining low employee turnover and high levels of operation performance
- Having fun

"Domino's Pizza had a culture that had evolved over a number of years. It measured success as doing just a little bit better each year than the previous year.

"Clearly, that kind of culture becomes dangerous over time, because while you are measuring success according to your own internal benchmarks and feeling pretty good about yourself, your competition can be kicking your butt.

"That was the case with Domino's when I arrived four years ago. We felt good about our record of steady same-store sales growth. But while we were growing a little, some of our competitors were growing a lot!

"We had lost market share for seven straight years in the pizza delivery category, and we had allowed certain competitors to become formidable while we were obsessed with our internal focus.

"I introduced Domino's to what I call the Wall Street mentality," says Brandon. "It meant we were going to benchmark ourselves against the very best in our category—and we couldn't declare victory until we beat them.

"We set our business objectives around growing market share and improving our operations as perceived by customers and independent research, not as perceived by us!

"I changed the leadership team by recruiting people who brought experiences and knowledge from other companies in the industry. We cut costs and redeployed capital to those areas of the business where we could create competitive advantages and gain customer support."

23

MICHAEL MASTERSON, CEO

Early to Rise

Be an impatient listener!

While many of the other CEOs interviewed for this book stressed the importance of listening, Michael Masterson expressed a contrary point of view.

Michael is a highly successful businessman—real estate and publishing—who has built a number of successful companies (including two with $100+ million annual sales). One of them is Early to Rise (http://www.earlytorise.com), a publisher of online newsletters and home study courses on business and success topics.

Michael says, "In a management newsletter, I read an article that said good leaders devote 80 percent of their communication time to listening, and that a good leader also helps people clarify and express their ideas by asking questions and restating what she hears the person say.

"Can you imagine spending 80 percent of your communication time listening? Listening to whom? Listening to what?

"If you spent that much time to listening, you'd soon be working away large chunks of your day hearing the same-old, same-old—mostly from grumblers and goof-offs.

"Yes, you would get the occasional good idea, but it wouldn't be worth it. Only a fool or a bureaucrat would devote so much of his productive time to such an unproductive exercise. Great leaders—individuals who have great ideas and the skill to persuade people to support them—are very frugal about their precious time.

"In fact most of the best and most admired leaders I know—and I'm thinking about theater directors, athletic coaches, and clergymen, as well as businesspeople—are impatient listeners. They will listen, but only to understand, not to mollify, humor, etc. As experienced businesspeople, they know that most of what is being said to them is irrelevant, superfluous, off-center, or dead wrong.

"Yes, they do make an effort to listen—they have to because their impulse is to not listen at all—but for the most part they want their conversations short and to the point. To spend an hour of a busy eight to ten hour day listening to some idea that can't work or a complaint that is unfounded feels like sheer idiocy to them.

"No, the problem with most management communication *isn't* poor listening; it's ineffective speaking. Effective speaking is like good writing—it is based on a good idea.

"When you have a good idea, you should say it as cleverly as you can. If you do then you will see the effect: people will take notice. They will get excited by it and—if you urge them to—they will work to support it.

"Here's something you won't hear from many other business experts: Most people most of the time *don't* have good ideas. In fact, most of what pass for ideas in business aren't really ideas at all. They are much more likely to be vague, emotionally laden reveries—with words attached—that they attempt to convey without analysis, consideration, and preparation.

"The newsletter article I referred to at the beginning said that by devoting some 80 percent of their communication time to listening-related activities, 'Leaders usually head off a great deal of the conflict that arises in companies when people feel no one is listening.' As if heading off conflict is the job of a leader! As if paying attention to problems would make them go away!

"If you want to be a good leader and a good communicator, learn these six strategies for practical listening:

1. If someone wants to vent, let him. But don't let him rant on. Give him about two minutes to make his case and then ask him, politely, to summarize his thoughts and feelings in a sentence or two.
2. Feel free to interrupt windbags and encourage them to state their point succinctly.
3. Listen to the literal meaning of what is being said, but pay attention also to the emotional message. In responding, address those emotional messages as well as the literal ones.

4. Break down every important conversation into component parts. Most discussions get derailed when the conversation flows from one subject to another and back again. Assign a 'title' to each major point—say, for example, 'John, we are talking about your salary now, is that right?' and then finish that conversation before you go on to the next.

5. Do not allow any individual point of discussion to take more than five or ten minutes to complete. Any time in excess of that is usually about the emotional issue, not the subject at hand. Treat the other person's time with respect and expect the same from him.

6. A few minutes before the end of the time you have allocated for the conversation, tell your interlocutor that you must stop talking and summarize the main points, identify what action needs to be taken, and, if necessary, schedule an additional conversation.

"If you can get yourself into the habit of doing these six things, you will not only save time and get more work done, you'll also impress those you speak to as a leader of exceptional intelligence and intellectual strength."

24

STEVAN ROBERTS, PRESIDENT
Edith Roman Associates

Take somebody who doesn't know how to do something,
show them how to do it, and give them credit for it.

"There's an old saying: 'Give a man a fish, feed him for a day; teach a man to fish, feed him for a lifetime.' My best leadership technique—take somebody who doesn't know how to do something, show them how to do it, and give them credit for it—is based on this principle," says Steve Roberts, president of Edith Roman Associates, one of the largest mailing list companies in the United States.

"For example, one of my account executives showed me an e-mail she was planning to send to an important client. The e-mail attempted to resolve a negotiation on pricing and terms, but was worded in an undiplomatic way that the client would surely have found offensive.

"I rewrote it in a more diplomatic way, e-mailed my version to my account executive, and suggested she send it using my version. But I didn't dictate to her which version to use, nor did I contact the client directly. I left it up to her.

"One of my key roles is to teach our people how to be successful in our business. I routinely accompany new account executives on sales calls so they can see how it is done. They learn to identify the client need, restate the need to the client, and close on the sale.

"A CEO cannot train everyone in a large organization personally. I select people, taking one person at a time under my wing.

"If someone does not work out, I prefer to let them go quickly. People have a calling, and if they are not suitable for your organization, they are suitable for someone else. You just make them miserable keeping them in an organization in which they will not succeed.

"Everybody screws up at one time or another. If you make a mistake, pick yourself up and move forward, and do not be afraid to take more risks. Without risk, there is no reward."

25

RONALD C. KESSELMAN, CEO AND CHAIRMAN

Elmer's Products, Inc.

Moderate your reactions to both good and bad news.

"I would say that powerful leadership is neither a complicated or complex issue," says Ron Kesselman of Elmer's.

"The most important piece of advice I would give is to be a steady leader. A key is moderating your reactions to both good and bad news. Have exactly the same temperament in both situations, and ask the same questions: What is the impact (e.g., financial, customers)? How can you moderate the downside or capitalize on the upside?

"For example, an Elmer's new product—wood fillers in clear tubes—far exceeded the sales forecast. However, this resulted in unacceptable customer service.

"The solution was to quickly expand the supply chain (which temporarily reduced profitability) while meeting with each customer to be sure they had minimum inventory requirements filled on an almost daily basis.

"After three months, we had increased production capacity and inventory levels. Both profitability and customer service were returned to normal levels.

"The result was that both ends of the problem were moderated: We continued to generate revenue from the sale of the new product without interruption in supply, while acceptable customer service levels were maintained. A side benefit (adversity often creates opportunities) was that we expanded the supplier base and reduced costs as vendors competed for the business.

"Leadership is neither an art form nor a management style. It is the result of a clear vision communicated throughout the organization, a high level of consistent performance, and unquestioned fairness and integrity. These are developed characteristics that can be significantly improved through hard work and being open to constructive feedback. One can develop a more receptive attitude toward constructive criticism with a combination of realistic self-appraisal and soliciting feedback from nonthreatening sources such as ex-colleagues."

26

BRUCE T. COLEMAN, CEO
El Salto Advisors

Lead by example.

"My most powerful leadership secret is to tell the truth and lead by example," says Bruce Coleman, CEO of El Salto Advisors. "There is an unfortunate tendency not to tell the truth, but being straight up helps people know where they stand and increases confidence in the leader."

"I had taken over a company on a Monday and had my first employee meeting on Tuesday. During the Q&A session, an employee asked if there might be layoffs.

"My answer was that because revenues had dropped precipitously, we would have no choice but to cut staff. I said that I would act quickly and fairly, but that there was no choice. When the person thanked me, I asked why. 'Because you are the first person to tell us the truth,' he said.

"A second company needed both leadership and a good example. I had asked the company to provide me a local apartment and rental car. The CFO called me before my arrival and asked if I would use the convertible my predecessor had used and his $8,500 a month apartment. My answer, of course, was hell no! My example was around the hallways in minutes, and everybody knew what I would expect from them."

Bruce offers the following advice on how to become a better leader:

- Ask your people how you can do better. Really listen, and do at least some of what they suggest.

- Periodically write yourself an honest report card and work on your weaknesses.
- Your brain or gut will nag you if something is not right. Learn to act on its message, no matter how difficult. Ignoring the warning will be at your peril.
- When faced with a difficult people issue, if all choices look reasonable, take the one that is personally most difficult to do. Reason: Often we avoid taking the correct step and rationalize why some other action is better. This maxim overcomes that tendency.
- Look to the advice of a respected person who has been in a situation similar to yours. "As a new CEO, I would have better served had I a mentor, rather than stumbling through the process of learning how to be a CEO and leader.

27

J. DARIUS BIKOFF, FOUNDER AND CEO

Energy Brands Inc.

It's all about being passionate and intense about what you do–and having fun at the same time.

"Integrating fun into the workplace has been key to my business's success," says Darius Bikoff, CEO of Energy Brands, the company that created the popular new enhanced waters, glacéau vitaminwater, and glacéau smartwater. "It's all about being passionate and intense about what you do . . . and having fun at the same time."

The label of the company's new glacéau vitaminwater flavor, leadership lemon rooibos tea, perhaps sums up Bikoff's leadership philosophy best:

> If "revenge of the nerds" movies have shown us anything, it's that corvette-driving, all-state quarterbacks with perfect bone structure, dandruff-free hair, and cheerleader girlfriends named Tiffany aren't true leaders.
>
> The real leaders are usually the dorky guys. The ones who were voted treasurer of the AV club, took their cousin to the prom, and spend most nights alone trying to watch the scrambled "nudie" channel.
>
> Now if that's the secret to success, no wonder a guy named Darius is our president.

Darius continues, "In the mid-1990s, when I was developing the concept for glacéau vitaminwater, I decided that in addition to being the pioneer in the enhanced water category, I wanted to create a product that consumers like me could connect with based on a fresh, modern approach that would be engaging.

"I decided to integrate fun and humor into every aspect of the company and give the brand a personality, something that had never quite been seen before in consumer products.

"From the label copy, voice mail recording, Web site, and trade show booth to the messages spontaneously scrawled on the glass walls in the office, I encouraged irreverence to be contagious.

"Today, the brand personality comes from the entire team's collective feedback and is projected into one idiosyncratic voice that can be heard on everything from our point of sale materials to our sampling vehicles. For example, two of the newest glacéau vitaminwater stickers read: 'Available in many colors, like a certain king of pop,' and 'How do you get the vitamins in the water? How do people get into Speedos?'

"While the sampling program GVWTV, for glacéau vitaminwater tasting vehicle, looks like a news truck, the crew, who are dressed like correspondents, enthusiastically spread the word about glacéau vitaminwater.

"This is symbolic of how glacéau vitaminwater overcame one of the greatest paradoxes in the beverage business—first by creating a product based on the science of healthy benefits while tasting great, and then by designing a somewhat clinical looking package that speaks a funny language. This adds an aesthetic to the brand, which is already considered by many experts to be the most elegant solution to the demand by modern consumers for healthier hydration options.

"Glacéau vitaminwater was the first brand to merge the obvious benefits of vitamins and water. The product was something I wanted for myself, and the big reward is that now millions of consumers every day let me know that I'm on the right track by buying a bottle.

"Glacéau vitaminwater resonates with so many people because it is intrinsically relevant to the healthier, more purposeful lifestyle we all lead. It simply makes perfectly good sense to choose a product that is low calorie, great tasting, and nutrient enhanced, in a package that is clean, modern, and straightforward with a personality that, at no additional cost, makes you laugh.

"I started in the business as a student. First of the biology of water, then of the beverage industry, and ultimately of my own brand. Now I am a teacher.

"I educate my team of over 450 people from across the country on a daily basis about the choice of being passionate and intense while having fun at the same time. In doing so, I hope to be following in the footsteps of other entrepreneurs before me who all redefined a category and achieved significant scale even in the face of extreme competition.

"For example, it wasn't Maxwell House but Howard Schultz at Starbucks who made coffee experiential. It wasn't IBM but Steve Jobs at Apple who made computers easier. And it wasn't British Airways but Richard Branson at Virgin who made flying enjoyable.

"Even in a highly evolved industry like beverages, by focusing on consumers like myself, I was able to create an innovative product and redefine bottled water. And by adding a dose of my secret ingredient, fun, glacéau vitaminwater is achieving significant scale."

28

WILLIAM P. LAUDER, COO
Estée Lauder

Clearly state the mission and objective of the company in a manner that gets everybody to understand and pull in that direction.

"The most important element of leadership is to clearly state the mission and objective of the company in a manner that gets everybody to understand and pull in that direction," says William Lauder of cosmetics giant, Estée Lauder. "Effective leaders communicate the objectives in a manner understandable by the audience they are talking to.

"Everybody sets the mission. It is not a directive from on high. It comes from the collective bottom up. When the mission is set in this fashion, everyone buys into it because they believe it is achievable.

"Estée Lauder is a large corporation with nineteen brands. I tell our employees that the organizational structure of Lauder is like the hierarchy of life in a pond that they learned about in high school biology.

"At the bottom are the amoebas. The tadpoles eat the amoebas and are higher up the hierarchy. The little fish eat the tadpoles. Big fish eat the little fish. Above the surface of the pond are the flies; the big fish eat the flies too.

"Our consumers are the flies. Our sales associates are the big fish in our organization's pond, because they represent the brand to the consumer. For the rest of us, our job is to make sure our big fish eat as many flies as possible, by creating powerful brands that attract flies.

"As the COO, I am the amoeba at the bottom of the pond. The consumer never sees me; she doesn't even know or care that I exist. My job is to create an environment where our people can build powerful brands.

"Each of the nineteen brands has its own unique mission. Everyone on our team must know what makes his or her brand special and unique.

"Clinique, for example, is allergy tested, fragrance free, dermatologist recommended. As far as the customer is concerned, the Clinique consultant in Bloomingdale's *is* the brand, because she is the person who interacts with the consumer.

"Your brand mission and statement cannot be overcommunicated. We reinforce our brand mantras constantly. Repetition and clarity are essential. I speak to different groups within the company two to three times a week, every week. I also have half a dozen informal conferences and meetings a week, and speak to hundreds of people at our sales force meetings. First and foremost, communication is key."

29

MASSIMO FERRAGAMO, CHAIRMAN
Ferragamo USA

*Select the best people for every key position, and give
them the authority necessary to do their jobs.*

"I believe in trying to master and develop the scence of selecting the
right people within an organization," says Massimo Ferragamo, "and
consequent to that, to be able to delegate and make them responsible
and the *owners* of what they are in charge of. When you entrust someone
and give them responsibility, you are automatically handing over a piece
of the company. It's up to him or her to live up to that ownership.

"As our company was prospering and growing, I think we selected
the best people for every key position, and we gave them all the authority necessary to do their jobs. More recently, we selected a president for
our company who was put into place, as I became chairman. I also
formed an executive committee with all of our top reports that meets
regularly and acts strongly together working as a team.

"The most important thing in selecting the right people is to first
have a clear understanding of their backgrounds, experience, and successes in previous companies, including their reputations in their industry. On top of this, it is essential to fit their strengths to the position they
will assume in the company.

"For this process, there are outside companies who specialize in
helping you determine this. In general, for me, the three most important criteria are: a person of high ethics, a strong business mind, and
someone who takes pleasure in the development of others.

"Some of the characteristics required to be a good leader include
being a team player, a coach, a strong people person; having a clear

focus for the task at hand and the capability of convincing others. If you like people, like to see others prosper, and enjoy working in a team, you might have the right qualities and can be a great leader.

"I think ultimately a great leader must be a people person. If you don't have that quality, you might get away with it for a few years, but for an all-around leader it is a necessary quality. I also suggest putting yourself at the service of the team, because it's the team who wins, not the coach.

"I don't know if good leadership is something you can learn, but you can get better at it. Also, one should remember that every day is a new learning process, and that you never stop learning."

30

DOROTHY CANN HAMILTON, FOUNDER AND CEO

The French Culinary Institute

Truly believe in the people you work with.

"My most powerful leadership skill is the ability to articulate and share a vision that people can believe in. But linked with that is my ability to truly believe in the people I work with. They have my trust as much as I have theirs," says Dorothy Cann Hamilton, founder and CEO of the French Culinary Institute.

"One of the more harrowing moments of my professional life was when the United Federation of Teachers, the teacher's union, tried to unionize our teachers. It was quite a shock and the most infuriating part was that I wasn't able to ask the teachers why they considered a union (it's part of the labor law regulating union elections).

"The best management techniques are always good communication. My instinct was just to talk to them. So, not knowing what could be their grievance and not being able to ask them, I just met with them, shared my vision, and asked them to believe in me, and in the fact that I would honestly listen to any concerns they had about the company.

"We met a few times with the faculty—just the COO and me. We told them we believed in them and hoped they believed in us. They did and the union was defeated.

"As the French Culinary Institute grew, my entrepreneurial skills were not enough to grow it into a first-class institution. In the process of striving for excellence, we needed to hire a COO.

"After much searching and trial and error, we found a terrific COO under our nose: our CFO. Gary Apito had worked with us for five years and did an outstanding job.

"For me to turn over my company, the one I founded and had nurtured for fifteen years, was difficult. But I had to believe in Gary and sent a clear message to the staff that he really was in charge of operations.

"I turned over my office, the corner and biggest office, and almost overnight had to watch him do things his way, not mine. I had to believe in him, more than I believed in myself. That was hard, but it was the best decision the company ever made.

"To be a good leader you must surround yourself with good people. Believe in them. Let them show you what they can do. Don't be overly critical, and remember to say thank you.

"The people you hire to work for you must share the same values and work ethic. They have to be excited about the product you are dealing with—in our case, is a cooking school.

"Our service is teaching people how to cook, so the people who work here must like working with people and also have to be excited by food. If people do not share our love of people and food, I don't care how committed they are, they will never understand my vision and values."

Dorothy offers some additional tips for becoming a more successful leader.

- Be sensitive to your customers. Treat them with real care. "A chef's job is to serve, to please people," she notes. (*Chef* means chief or leader.)
- Balance your work with your personal life. "You need a life other than your business," says Dorothy, who is married and has a nine-year-old daughter.
- Be resilient. "No one has ever run a business without bumps. The great test is whether you can bounce back."
- Invest time and love in those people who give you resilience.
- A great leader is a generalist, not a specialist. "To be a good leader you must develop a lot of different skill sets, versus just having one or two specialties. You have to be well-rounded."
- Keep in touch with yourself. Stay grounded and level.

Focus not on yourself, but on the effect you have on other people, from your direct reports to your customers.

31

PAUL G. GARRITY, SR., CEO
Garrity Industries, Inc.

Practice.

"I've often heard a real leader is a man who can build a firm foundation with the bricks that others throw at him," says Paul G. Garrity. "However, a true leader builds respect from his actions. He must be both confident as well as modest.

"There are so many characteristics that make a person a good leader: a leader should be authentic, a listener, stand for values, lead by example, be honest, provide direction, and—most important—be daring, take risks, and develop and empower others. This combination of techniques is what makes a true leader.

"After working for several companies from the lowest level to top management, I decided to risk starting my own consumer products company. My first company introduced a new concept in cigarette lighting. The product was a cigarette lighter that eliminated messy refilling by using a drop in cartridge refill. This company grew to the #2 position in the industry within three years.

"I subsequently founded a company to produce and market a disposable cigarette lighter. This was a daring new concept never before seen in the North American market. Success breeds competition, and soon two major companies copied the idea. Today disposable lighters enjoy approximately 80 percent of the market.

"My present company was born with another new concept: a disposable flashlight. A daring idea whose success led to the introduction of a complete line of new and exciting refillable flashlights and lanterns.

"Today Garrity Industries has several plants in the USA and Canada, as well as the Orient and Europe. Despite the fact that our competitors have many more years of experience, Garrity maintains the major market share in our industry. We are known as an innovator and leader in product design and development, which has helped us to grow in a rather traditional industry.

"Perhaps the best way for a person to learn how to become a leader is to implement it; it should be practiced the same way a great athlete achieves his goal."

32

MICHAEL FLEISCHER, CEO
Gartner, Inc.

Open, informal communication fosters teamwork and success.

"I believe that open, informal communication within a company fosters teamwork, collaboration, and success. I use a variety of techniques to insure that this type of communication happens at all levels of the company," says Michael Fleischer, CEO of Gartner, Inc.

"You must get to know people on a personal level if you are going to work effectively with them. You need to understand their values, their goals, and their motivation if you want to make them as productive and successful as possible. People need a chance to express their views in an informal, unthreatening setting if you want to understand what really makes them tick.

"My favorite technique is 'Lunch at Colony Grill.' I regularly meet one-on-one with each member of my team for an informal lunch. The venue is always the Colony Grill, one of Stamford's finest low-end restaurants. Located in a gritty, industrial area of the city, Colony serves outstanding thin-crust pizza in an earthy, casual, and utterly unpretentious environment.

"This meeting is not about getting things done! That's what we spend our time doing all day, every day at the office. This meeting is about having time to explore and reflect so that the time we spend trying to get things done in the office is more productive, focused, and enjoyable.

"The idea is to meet without any specific agenda in a very unbusinesslike setting, far removed from the rhythms and pressures of the office. The environment fosters open talk about life and work on a personal level that rarely seems to happen around the office. You learn what really matters to people, and they learn what really matters to you. Deep connections occur that facilitate valuable, ongoing working relationships.

"I also hold regular forums throughout the company where associates are free to ask any questions of me whatsoever. When we hold all-company meetings, I solicit anonymous questions through a confidential e-mail box to remove any fear associates might have about asking the tough questions that are really on their mind.

"While it is critical to foster good internal communication, every business ultimately exists to meet the needs of customers. As a leader, you are tasked with overseeing what can be an enormously complex operation, which can easily involve thousands of people all over the world. You constantly find yourself being asked to make tough judgments about policy changes and resource allocation.

"The only way you can lead with authority and credibility in this sort of environment is to know your customer better than anyone else in the organization. By regularly spending time with a broad cross-section of customers, you are able to insure that the organization avoids getting wrapped up in its own concerns, and that it remains steadfastly focused on giving the customers what they want.

"I want to understand our customers better than any other executive in the company. CEOs are always hearing from the other executives about what customers want as a means of justifying some sort of action, or in many cases, some sort of inaction. If the CEO really has an accurate pulse on customer needs, he will be in a strong position to drive resources to areas that really matter most to customers."

33

JOHN GOODMAN, CEO

The Goodman Group

Intuition, intelligence, and passion.

John Goodman of The Goodman Group of companies says that his most powerful leadership secret is "using intuition to identify opportunity, intelligence to understand it, and passion to act on it.

"*Intuition* is the inner voice. It's a sense of knowing opportunity, without immediate proof of how you know. It's a leap from problem to solution, which transcends usual thought processes. Everyone is born with intuition; it's God talking to us between our thoughts.

"*Intelligence* is the unique ability and creativity of yourself and the people with whom you work, and how you work together. Intelligence is the collective wisdom that enables us to effectively act on opportunity.

"*Passion* is truly caring about what you do, and doing it. Passion is what transitions opportunity to success.

"The synergy between intuition, intelligence, and passion is the foundation of The Goodman Group's success.

"When I started in the senior living and health care business more than 30 years ago, we owned a handful of nursing homes. Over the years, we became known for our outstanding medical care; state surveyors consistently gave our nursing homes exceptionally high ratings.

"Every nursing home and retirement community at that time was based on a medical model, not a residential model. We were turning a profit. The state was happy. Our partners were happy. The families of our residents were happy. Why do more?

"Intuitively, I believed we had an obligation to do more than just care for residents physically, even if it would cost us more money, more time, and more labor. Even if we didn't have to make the extra effort, I felt we were morally obligated to do so. It's within these moral choices that intuition whispers and true opportunity awaits.

"The issue came to the forefront shortly after I started leading The Goodman Group back in the early '70s. I was visiting one of our Montana senior living communities when the administrator expressed her concern about what seemed to be a lingering depression among some of the residents. The usual activities—tea, outings to restaurants, and musical entertainment—didn't seem to bring them out of their funk.

"With intuition, the inner voice whispers, and when it's true, you'll hear it answered in some of the least-expected ways. Within a couple of days, the administrator received a call from the local school district. They were interested in having some nursing-home residents read to their elementary school students. The residents loved the idea. They visited the school several times a month to lead story-times, and were transformed from being achy, unhappy, and depressed to joyous and brimming with zest for life.

"The program planted a seed of an idea. Intergenerational programming—giving seniors the opportunity to interact with people of all ages, be a part of the larger community, and have purpose in life—was key to helping them stay emotionally and spiritually healthy.

"It wasn't long thereafter this seed took root, through The Palms of Largo in Largo, Florida. We had just purchased a 732-unit rental property called Imperial Palms. Right next-door were 54 unfinished foundations by a homebuilder who was eager to sell.

"I had a vision of expanding Imperial Palms into a hospitality and wellness-based model for senior living. A place where seniors could receive care and services in a residential, hotel-like setting, as opposed to a skilled-nursing setting.

"It would be far more than a residence; it would be a place where people could have a sense of community and live among people of all ages. It was a radical idea back then. But when intuition is valid, you'll find that others will be thinking about the same concept, no matter how unconventional.

"About that time, two of our most experienced and successful nursing home administrators—who had never discussed their idea with each other and lived thousands of miles apart—wanted to try a then unheard-of concept: assisted living, where seniors receive services in their own apartment. The three of us virtually had the same idea of hospitality-based service simultaneously.

"The intelligence we had gained from years in the senior living industry enabled us to respond to this intuition effectively, efficiently, and confidently. We could have simply continued business as usual and chosen not to innovate. After all, we were turning a profit. But our passion for service simply would not allow us to maintain the status quo.

"The result? Two pioneering assisted living programs in Oregon and Portland, and what we believe may be the nation's first intergenerational living community—The Palms of Largo. This 96-acre community serves more than 1,700 people, ages six weeks to well over 80 years.

"It offers a learning center, independent living, assisted living, memory centers, and skilled nursing care in several beautifully designed residences. It features a holistic health spa and wellness center, even a Zen garden, and one of the nation's few skilled nursing centers designed especially for children. The Goodman Group cannot lay claim that we invented assisted living; however, we certainly were among the very first.

"If we were a public company that had to answer to typical stockholders, The Palms of Largo may not exist. They would demand that we do only what was necessary to provide service and turn a profit.

"We had little more than intuition and a bit of empirical evidence that a hospitality-based, intergenerational senior living concept would be a success. You'll be hard-pressed to find stockholders who will put their faith in anything based on such scant proof—I often wonder how this mindset undermines opportunities or sidetracks organizations into unsuccessful ventures.

"Over and over, experience has taught me that intuition, intelligence, and passion can cultivate the seeds of opportunity into a harvest of success and good will."

John's advice for learning to become a better leader is to "know yourself—your mind, body, and spirit. This will help you to make the most of your gifts, develop areas of weakness and, most importantly, give you the power to create the life you really want rather than simply reacting. By knowing yourself, you'll free yourself to act with wisdom, not pride or ignorance or fear.

"Remember, what you think is what you create. By knowing what you want out of life, by knowing your abilities, you will be able to envision your dreams, and make them come true. You won't fight situations. Instead, you'll have the strength to use your intuition, intelligence and passion to respond wisely."

34

ED NUSBAUM, EXECUTIVE PARTNER AND CEO

Grant Thornton

Identify what makes your organization unique.

"My key leadership secret is to identify what makes an organization unique or better, formulate this difference into a vision, build a strategy around the vision, execute on the strategy, and constantly communicate the vision and strategy to everyone within the organization," says Ed Nusbaum, CEO of Grant Thornton, a global accounting, tax, and business advisory organization.

This differentiation can be based on a product, service, niche, or market space. Some marketers call this the Unique Selling Proposition, or USP—the single factor that makes you different or better than the competition.

Grant Thornton differentiates itself based on a niche, according to Ed, who says the firm focuses on serving midsize companies. "Specifically, our vision is to be recognized as the leading business advisor and accounting firm serving midsize companies.

"But your strategy can evolve and move," he adds, noting that Grant Thornton is now taking on larger clients as well as midsize companies.

To implement the strategy, Ed says, you must give individuals within the organization responsibility for making sure certain goals are met, and establish criteria for measuring performance.

"If you are not a 'born leader,' you can develop your leadership abilities through training and experience," he says. Leaders must be able to build consensus within a team. "To be an effective managing partner, I need the support of the other partners."

While a leader must be a team player, he or she must also be strong-willed, and forceful enough to make unpopular decisions.

"For example, in the wake of the scandal surrounding Enron and its accounting firm Arthur Anderson, the partners at Grant Thornton were not sure that we should speak out on how to restore the public trust in the accounting profession through leadership," Ed says.

"They were concerned that we would get caught in the cross fire. But we took a proactive position, and in fact hired 500 people from Anderson, including 60 partners. Since the Enron scandal, we have posted 25 percent annual growth."

He concludes: "You never have all the answers. An executive must constantly develop to become a better leader and grow as time goes on."

35

RAY BARTON, CEO AND CHAIRMAN OF THE BOARD

Great Clips, Inc.

Create a vision everyone in the organization understands,
supports, and works to achieve.

"The most powerful leadership tool I have found is creating a vision everyone in the organization understands, supports, and works to achieve. When everyone in the organization supports the vision it makes decisions easier because there is a clear focus. People begin to think long term and are willing to accept short-term investments of time and money to make the long-term vision a reality," says Ray Barton, CEO of Great Clips, Inc.

Great Clips, headquartered in Minneapolis, is North America's largest and fastest-growing hair salon brand in the $50-billion hair-care industry. Established in 1982, Great Clips has perfected a system for delivering competitively priced, high-quality haircuts and perms to men, women, and children. The company began franchising in 1983, and today, nearly 1,900 Great Clips salons operate in 85+ markets across the United States and Canada.

At the company's first convention in 1988, when the organization was six years old, Barton, in his opening speech put up a slide that said:

3,000 by 2000
Great Clips Leads the Hair-Care
Industry into the 21st Century

Great Clips is a 3,000-salon hair-care chain with operations
coast-to-coast and annual sales in excess of $1,000,000,000.

Ray explains, "At the time, we had less than 200 salons open, no real plan, no money, and no business talking about 3,000 salons. We knew our industry would change and someday, someone would have 3,000 salons under one brand. Why not us? Our goal was always to be the leader, the best, and the biggest.

"People throughout our organization began to talk about 3,000 salons. At first people talked about how impossible and unrealistic the dream was. We kept talking and dreaming and using the vision *3,000 by 2000* in all of our communications. Soon everyone was talking about what we needed to do to make our dream a reality. Our conversations and the way we thought as an organization changed.

"In January of 1990, we held a franchisee meeting called '5 to 50.' The meeting was to help franchisees develop business plans to grow. Only select, invited franchisees attended.

"At the end of the meeting we presented a more detailed vision for our organization in the form of a mock *Wall Street Journal* article dated July 13, 1999. It described how we would look ten years in the future. The franchisees attending signed the article and many put a number by their name indicating the number of salons they would open. They now owned a piece of the 3,000-salon dream.

"Vision is the dream of what can be. Creating the picture and making it come alive in people's minds helps focus efforts toward making the dream come true. Having a clear picture of where you are going and what you want to be helps people understand why they are working so hard. It is not work for money; it is work to create something, to do something others could not do and thought was impossible. Very exciting. Very powerful.

"*3,000 by 2000* was our vision. Everyone believed in our vision and that we could make it real. It changed the way we did business and the way we dealt with each other.

"By establishing our vision, and making it very simple, measurable, and clear, we created a team effort to make it real. Great Clips, Inc., and the franchisees made huge investments of money, time, and effort. The dream helped us set priorities and make decisions.

"We haven't yet opened our 3,000th salon, but we will; our timing was just a little off. Because we had a dream, we are now North America's largest and fastest growing salon brand, and we truly believe we are the best.

"We currently have 1,900 salons, and will have over 2,000 by the end of the year. We will open over 250 salons this year, and will reach our goal of 3,000 salons.

"Great Clips is recognized throughout the industry as the industry leader. Our vision is the same, but the words we use to communicate have changed to 'Clearly #1 . . . The Dominant Haircare Brand.' Our vision drives our every decision.

"Thinking long term is part of creating a vision. From the very beginning, we had a strategy to develop only a few markets at a time. We did this so we could afford to support our franchisees and they would have the marketing necessary to build our brand and to separate themselves from the local competition.

"Shortly after we began franchising, a prospective franchisee from a market that we were not currently developing sent us a signed agreement and a check for the $10,000 franchisee fee. We had no way to attract additional franchisees in the market. No support system was established, and we had several markets that we needed to continue to develop before adding new ones. We needed the $10,000, and it would have made things easier in the short term; but it most likely would have caused problems for us in the long term. We sent the check back because we believed in our strategy and long-term thinking.

"Leadership is difficult to define and even more difficult to learn. I have studied leaders and tried to learn how they were able to create a vision and then lead people to make that vision their own. A leader must have a strong belief in themselves and the willingness to take huge personal risks by throwing a stake in the ground, stating their vision, and continuing to communicate the vision even when it seems impossible and others doubt. The communication must be consistent and constant, and the leader's actions must support the vision."

36

TRANUM FITZPATRICK, CEO

Guilford Capital Corporation (GCI)

Lead from the front.

Tranum Fitzpatrick of GCI believes that the most powerful of all the elements of leadership is to "lead from the front."

"To me this means that—always keeping in mind that you are the leader of a team and not an actor—you must:

- Determine the business principles which will define your company.
- Closely communicate those principles to your people, then keep finding new ways of continually communicating those same principles.
- Then you yourself always abide by these principles.

"Simple? Yes. Always easy? No. Powerful? Very.

"Be aware that, over the course of your career, you are going to encounter periods of business crises—some of them probably very great crises. When those crises occur, it is critical that, while letting your people know that you recognize the crisis, you maintain a demeanor of calmness and of the assurance that 'we are going to come through this.'

"A recent example occurred in March, during a record cold snap in our part of the country. Two of the most important principles of our company quickly came to the fore in this crisis, principles that are known to everyone in our company, including our regular contractors. They are:

- Always put the best interest of the customer first.
- The job descriptions of everyone in our company all start with the same phrase: 'Whatever it takes.'

"At 5:10 AM on a Thursday morning, I got a call from Tom Latimer, our partner in three buildings in a city 100 miles from our office, including a fifteen-story downtown residential building. It was hard to hear Tom for the incessant ringing of the fire alarm. Tom had gotten a call at his home from the alarm company 45 minutes earlier, called Brian Crawford, our maintenance chief for all three buildings, and gone directly to the building where they learned, that, in the record cold, a sprinkler line on the 14th floor had burst, pumping out an inch and a quarter stream of water.

"The fire department, following their procedures, would not allow us to shut off the system until they had inspected each and every room in the fifteen-story (plus basement) building to determine that there was no evidence of fire. This procedure, because a number of apartment residents were out of town and because a bank occupies the first floor, took over 2½ hours.

"During this entire time, the pump pushed water through the break, onto the floor, down the hallway, and into the elevator shafts. We estimate that, due to a metal lip at each floor, about 60 percent of the water that ran into each shaft 'got off' at the 13th floor and ran down that hallway until it reached a depth of roughly eight to twelve inches—a level at which the water pressure became sufficient to hold the rest of the water in the shaft, a process to be repeated on each successive floor.

"To return to the hallways, that water was rushing three ways: under the apartment doors, where it flooded the apartments; down the interior stairwells, where it began to freeze; and out the outside fire escapes, where it really froze! Meanwhile, as the 14th floor apartments got flooded, water began to pour through the ceilings of the 13th floor apartments, just as those apartments were being flooded by water pouring under their doors, a process repeated on each floor.

"The alarm wouldn't stop ringing. The power was off, except for the emergency lights, the alarm, and the pump. There was ice on the stairs. And the elevators didn't work. It would be very difficult to exaggerate the extent of this problem.

"Normally, one call to Howard Upchurch, president of our development and management company would have gotten this off my plate. But Howard was on his way to catch a plane.

"Britt Bender, asset manager for this property, was leaving shortly for Louisiana with Bill Porter, a building consultant who had worked with us for over 25 years. One phone call and they'd changed and were on their way to Watts.

"Fred Clifford is vice president of F&C Construction, which often does work for us and does it well. In 30 minutes, he was on his way to Watts with a full crew following right behind. Wylene Craft, who is always great in a crisis, assembled a three-person team headed by her, and they were on their way to Watts within an hour and a half. Tom and Brian were there and stayed there.

"Together, they did it all:

- They looked after the customers first, as always. We had more than one set of customers—in this case three sets: our investors, our lenders, our tenants.
- They did whatever it took. What could have been an absolute disaster was handled beautifully by good people following sound principles.

"It seems to me that the best way to become a better leader is through a combination of reading, observation, and application. Books such as this one are highly valuable opportunities to learn. All of us are exposed almost daily to different styles of leadership. Become a keen observer. What seems good to you? What seems false? Then try the ones that seem good, and put your own stamp on them."

37

IRWIN SIMON, CEO
Hain Celestial Group

Communicate.

"Hain Celestial is the world's largest natural food and organic product company. We have literally gone from zero sales and zero employees, to approximately $700 million in annual sales with 2,000 employees," says CEO Irwin Simon.

"My most powerful leadership strategy is to communicate. I have no hidden agendas. We have four clear messages in our company: build brands, stick to strategy, have good people, and achieve financial goals.

"In my opinion, too many people hide behind e-mail as a way to avoid personal, face-to-face communication. E-mail and voice mail are the easy way out when there's something important to talk about. They hurt communication by eliminating the need to speak to the person directly.

"Once every quarter, I visit all of our locations in the U.S., Canada, and Europe to talk to all of our employees. I tell them the good and bad in the company. I also spend a lot of time in one-on-one meetings with my direct reports.

"You can't lead by hiding behind a computer screen. When the leader is out there on the plant floor, people know that you care.

"Don't be afraid to be open, honest, and frank. If there is a problem, say what you think about it. It is not important that you be liked, although that's nice; it is important that the people in your organization respect you.

"When people communicate, good ideas are heard and acted upon. The people who have the best ideas are often those who work with customers or make the product, not the executives sitting at computers in the company headquarters.

"Once, when I was visiting one of our manufacturing plants, the floor people showed me that our machines could be used to package beverages other than teas. As a result, we branched out into lattes and ciders.

"In another plant, we were making organic baby food. The manufacturing people showed me that the same machines could bottle small jars of soup, and we got the idea of selling organic soups made in the same plant.

"A balanced life is important. People have two sides to them—work and their personal life. We try to help our people have fun at work for eight hours, and live good lives at home."

38

SY SPERLING, FOUNDER AND PRESIDENT (RETIRED)
Hair Club for Men (HCM)

Realize your own shortcomings.

"What helped me was one powerful idea—to realize my own short-comings and tap into the creativity and expertise of others to fill the gaps in my own knowledge and abilities."

When Sy Sperling started the Hair Club for Men, he had a partner who tried to do everything himself, because he thought no one was smarter than him. "His detriment and the cause of his failure was that he did not realize his own shortcomings. I succeeded by seeing what he did wrong and avoiding his mistakes," says Sy.

Sy recommends finding people who know more than you. "Law-yers, ad agencies, accountants—tap into them. Pick their brains. Hire them. You do not have to reinvent the formula for success. Just find out what it is and model it.

"Buying a franchise is a great way for an entrepreneur to make money from someone else's success formula. At the Hair Club for Men, half of our locations were company-owned, and half were franchised. By buying a franchise like HCM or McDonald's, you are buying their success formula, and increasing your own odds of making your business a success.

"You can overcome any shortcoming. What you don't know can be learned from other people. Find an expert who knows more than you do, and pick his brains for an afternoon or for a day.

"My other favorite leadership principle is to learn to relate to peo-ple, especially the average guy in the street. I would always talk to our employees—from the executives to the lowest levels—build a relationship, and kid around with them.

"At one time I thought HCM had outgrown my abilities to manage it, and I brought in a corporate guy to run things. I told him it was important to spend time in our locations to learn the business. But he never left his office, never got into the trenches. He failed as a result.

"Being smart is valuable, but people skills are even more important. Look at Bush and Gore. Gore is a an intellectual with a high IQ; Bush is of average intelligence, and now Bush is president of the United States."

39

DR. THOMAS F. FRIST, JR., CHAIRMAN EMERITUS
HCA

*Surround yourself with good people who balance
out your weaknesses with their strengths.*

"My most important leadership principle was surrounding myself with good people who balanced out my strengths and weaknesses," says Thomas Frist, MD, who in 1968 cofounded HCA in Nashville, Tennessee.

"For instance, my strength was not operations. So I hired Jack Bovender, who had a proven track record, great ethics, and strong moral character, as our COO.

"From 1978 to 1984, we built the best board in corporate America. In 1997, I came back to a $20 billion company as CEO and let 12 of the top 16 officers go in the first month, because of either their management style, abilities, or the public's lack of trust in them. They were identified with all of the problems associated with a massive government investigation into fraud and abuse. Over the next six months an outstanding senior management team was assimilated that represented both the skills and values necessary to lead a healthcare company with 270,000 employees.

"I also rebuilt the board again to one of the best in the United States. Several members have been recognized by 'Corporate Board' as Directors of the Year."

Thomas most admires Ronald Reagan as a great leader. Other advice from him for leaders includes:

- Stay focused.
- Don't take on too many tasks at once.
- Prioritize.
- Observe, read about, and study the lives of successful leaders in many different sectors.
- Always remain true to your word.

40

CARLETON S. FIORINA, CEO

Hewlett-Packard (HP)

*We have a responsibility to redefine the role of
the corporation on the world stage.*

"As leaders, now more than ever before, we have a responsibility to redefine the role of the corporation on world stage, and to leverage our ability to impact individuals, companies, communities, nations for the better," says Carly Fiorina, CEO of Hewlett-Packard.

"We must remake our businesses to be far more active corporate citizens—creators not only of shareowner value, but also of social value, in ways that are systemic and sustainable.

"It becomes our job to use a profit engine to raise the capabilities, extend the hopes, and extinguish despair across the globe.

"We have a chance and an imperative to improve the choices, economic condition, and sphere of opportunity for billions more people here at home and around the globe. It's a greater mandate, one that our customers increasingly demand on us, one that is deserved by every country in which we do business, and one, I'd argue, that must be undertaken because it can be undertaken.

"This is a mandate that started as a quiet whisper more than a decade ago, and more recently could be heard loudly in Seattle and Prague and Genoa in the voices of protesters who declare that global companies have not lived up to their responsibilities.

"What is important here is not to take sides in the globalization debate, but to look at the problem and work toward a real solution.

"As the world moves toward a knowledge economy, the mandate for leadership changes.

"Unlike a world dominated solely by manufacturing prowess or distribution reach—one in which success is often about wringing cost out of the system or maximizing a supply chain—we've entered a different world.

"In a knowledge economy, an economy driven by intellectual and human capital, in addition to financial and physical capital, the transfer of knowledge, information, and know-how—the exchange of services—will become an increasingly important driver.

"In such an economy, partnership, trust, reliability, and respect become important. Which is why, in an economy where intellectual capital is currency, corporate behavior becomes a scorecard by which you are judged—by your customers, your employees, and your shareowners.

"That scorecard will, of course, include your ability to be a competitive player, but equally important on the score-card will be:

- Your integrity and your character
- Your ability to transfer value and know-how into local economies in which you do business
- Your track-record as a socially responsible corporate citizen
- Your ability to sustain and nurture true partnerships and ecosystems in which all parties gain both social good and economic gain

"The winning companies of this century will be those who prove with their actions that they can be profitable and increase social values—companies that both do well and do good. So much so, in fact, that business leaders will no longer view doing well and doing good as separate pursuits, but as one unified pursuit.

"And, increasingly, shareowners, customers, partners, and employees are going to vote with their feet—rewarding those companies that achieve social change through business.

"The companies that will be worthy of their investment, money, time, and energy will be those with similar values and those that can meet a much higher standard of performance.

"I should note this has nothing to do with politics or subscribing to a particular ideology or economic theory. This is simply the new reality of business—one that we should and must embrace.

"The question, of course, is, how?

"Whether your business, like HP's, spans the entire globe, or just the eight blocks around this building, the same principles apply.

"There are key leadership imperatives that are at work, and must be mastered, for all of us as leaders to operate and succeed going forward.

"Imperative number one is the principle of leadership and the mandate to build a winning culture. This first leadership imperative starts within the walls of your company, in the vision you set and in the culture you build.

"Recently, in the business world we talked about culture as a lever for change and a means of motivating employees—and, certainly, that's still true. But particularly since September 11, culture has also come to mean something else.

"According to a recent *Wall Street Journal* article on the redefinition of the workplace in light of recent events: 'The tragedy brought need for safety, security, belonging, and affiliation into sharp relief.'

"Clearly, it is leadership's responsibility to give employees space and support to rethink their priorities in the wake of recent events. But the article goes on to say that if 'managed correctly, recent events present an opportunity to strengthen employees' sense of affiliation through a vision, a common mission, a common sense of purpose.'

"In this context, as leaders, we must answer the question for our employees: In a world where know-how and insight and intelligence and inventive spirit are the keys to success, what role will our company play in fostering it, and what role will we play in harnessing it?

"Once we answer this, we then have to foster a culture that can deliver on that vision.

"It's important to remember that top leaders can set a vision, set a strategy, set a system of rewards and metrics that encourage people, reward people, and train people. But the rest is ultimately up to the individuals and teams in our companies. It is very much the acts of individuals, the every day acts of many, which make the biggest difference in the overall performance of a company."

41

PERNILLE LOPEZ, PRESIDENT

IKEA North America

*The greatest privilege of leadership is to guide
people toward the path to achieve great things.*

IKEA's Pernille Lopez says that one thing she has learned as a leader is that it's important to have courage and dare to be yourself, "To take risks, step out of the comfort zone and lead the way. To see the landscape that is constantly changing as exciting, not a threat. Embrace it, and it will lead to new places with new challenges and opportunities. It's easy to have courage when you have the sails in the winds. It's important to find out if you still have courage when there are tough times.

"Leadership for me represents what I stand for as a person. I stand for passion. People who know their passion and follow it are successful. A work colleague once asked my advice about taking on the 'next step.' At the time she was an interior decorator in my store, and the only next step she could see was becoming a department manager. I asked her, 'What is your passion? ' Today, she's one of our best interior decorators and works with all of our stores in North America. The powerful results that can come in pursuit of your passion are only possible when you stick with it, even when it's ugly, when there are tough times and things are falling apart. If you don't have that passion, and the tenacity to stick with it no matter what, you start questioning yourself and the people around you."

Pernille goes on to say, "Trust—I stand for trust. You don't have to earn my trust; I will give it to you. It's amazing what happens in relationships when they come from trust. Trust sets people free. We suddenly become honest with each other and empowered. As a leader it's a lot more motivating for me to run a business when I am not being second-guessed or controlled all of the time, and I've seen how this approach can have a tremendous impact on the dynamics of your work relationships. I have performed my best as a leader, as a wife, as a friend, and as mother when trust has been given to me. I have also seen the difference it makes even in your children when you give them trust. As a leader, trust can really be demonstrated by the simple act of maintaining an open-door policy and ensuring that coworkers know that no matter what level they are, they can count on me to be available and easily accessible.

"And finally, I stand for commitment. As a leader you have to be committed to sustain support and go all the way at 100 plus percent, especially when there are challenges. When others are ready to jump ship because things are hard or complicated or confusing, those are the times to stand tall and be committed to your own passions and values. This is also when courage is necessary to demonstrate to fellow coworkers, whether a business issue or personal issues may be affecting their work efforts, that you consistently stand behind them no matter what, which helps to firmly establish trust. That's when as a leader your example will be followed. When there's too much to do, people will rise to the occasion to do more. When it's time to transform vision into reality, there will be many willing to support change. That's what enables people to achieve great things. And for me, that's one of the greatest privileges of leadership—to guide people toward the path to achieve great things."

42

WILLIAM T. MONAHAN, CHAIRMAN AND CEO

Imation Corp.

Lead by example.

"The most important leadership technique I know of is to lead by example," says William Monahan of Imation, specialists in data storage. "We hear a lot about 'walk the talk,' 'get out front,' and so on, but we don't always see as much of it as would be effective.

"Everyone in a company watches what the leader or CEO does, where they go, how they travel, do they communicate, do they practice what they preach. Employees then determine the credibility of a leader based on the consistency of his or her actions.

"I am particularly against CEO perks such as limos, corporate aircraft, huge offices, special treatment. These perks set leaders apart from the team. They create the 'Star CEO' syndrome and cause a disconnect from reality.

"I also believe strong leaders need to set an example in being able to say no. It is very important to avoid or eliminate effective or nonsuccessful programs and projects. Often companies allow those to continue drawing resources, attention, and focus from priorities.

"Employees respect a definitive *no*. It is also crucial that leaders can say no to customers when the deal or the direction negatively impacts the company's financial success. *No* often establishes the right atmosphere in tough sales situations, gets the truth in front on the customer, and leads to a win-win.

"At Imation, we did not create perks. We believe the entire team should work together, without special perks for executives. This has allowed us to take on divestitures, restructuring, and downsizing, and maintain the morale and dedication of our employees. We set policies, and executives follow the same policies.

"Also crucial is to explain to all employees not just what we are doing, but why and what will change due to these actions. You get a much faster response and better understanding with all employees pulling in the same direction if the why is outlined.

"An example of both walking the talk and providing the why of a decision occurred at Imation recently. We closed down part of a business operation affecting 15 employees. I personally announced the actions to the team affected and why we had to take these steps.

"We received numerous e-mails thanking us for meeting face-to-face and taking responsibility for the decision and outlining why we had to do it. The result was that the affected employees enjoyed a smooth transition. We ended up cooperating with another company to hire them, and we are referring business to them.

"A person who has good leadership capability can become better by consistent training and input. They need to gather new input and layout an improvement plan. One of the best techniques is to agree with a mentor who is the best leader in the organization and learn from that person, striving to be as good as them or better.

"If someone has leadership shortcomings, the only answer is admission and realization that the shortcomings are theirs. Without employees understanding that improvement is needed, they will be in denial and not improve.

"Using unbiased, independent mentoring and training has been successful in improving these types of leaders, but not in more than 50 percent of the cases. Denial is tough to overcome."

43

DR. ULRICH SCHUMACHER, CEO

Infineon Technologies

Dare to be different.

"Dare to be different," urges Ulrich Schumacher of Infineon. "It is easy for managers to simply administer their responsibilities and meet expectations. Real leadership, however, requires a pioneering spirit and the courage to take risks. You've got to have the competitive drive to take on challenges that other colleagues think are almost impossible—and then pursue your vision of the future realistically but relentlessly.

"As a young man, I worked my way up through the ladder of Siemens Corporation, armed with an engineering Ph.D., by volunteering to take on struggling areas of the business that I believed could be turned around in two years. Because traditional corporate culture tends to discourage entrepreneurial risk-taking, relatively few people were interested in associating themselves challenging projects.

"In the mid-1990s I was given a high degree of freedom to turn the Siemens semiconductor memory and standard IC division around. Of course, there were many challenges along the way, but with a dedicated team working hard we were able to deliver success where other people saw only obstacles.

"Siemens eventually decided to spin off its semiconductor division into a separate company called Infineon. In March 2000, with the worldwide markets at their peak, we were listed on the Frankfurt and New York Stock Exchange. Our stock price more than tripled in that environment of exaggerated valuations, but amid all the dot-com and IT industry hype few people could have known that a few months later the semiconductor industry was about to begin the most dramatic downturn in its history.

"It is important to understand that the semiconductor industry is volatile even in the best of times. We have the highest average annualized growth (15 percent) of any industry over the past 40 years (by comparison, the second fastest growing industry, pharmaceutical, averages only 10 percent). But we experience steep downturns and recoveries that occur 8 to 12 months ahead of the rest of the economy.

"When the storm clouds began to appear on the horizon in the fall of 2000, I knew from experience we could not afford to be complacent. Infineon is a $5 billion dollar company, with 30,000 patents and more than 30,000 employees worldwide.

"Coming off strong annual revenue growth of 72 percent in 2000, I was determined that we would make tough decisions proactively from a position of strength—doing whatever it took to cut costs, maintain our financial solidity, and concentrate on our core competencies—ensuring that Infineon remained at the leading edge of the semiconductor industry.

"Counter to traditional European management models, I decided that Infineon would not mortgage its future by seeking savings in reduced research and development budgets. By thinking differently and acting aggressively, Infineon was able to continue to significantly invest in the development of new technology.

"Our decision to improve productivity while cutting costs in the early days of the worldwide downturn saved Infineon. The initiative, known as Impact, was a rapid reaction to the worst market slump, and achieved about 2.8 billion euro in cash-effective cost reduction, and more than 1.3 billion euro in EBIT-effective savings in record time. These strong cost-cutting measures also required the cutting of over 5,500 jobs worldwide on the heels of a company-wide expansion.

"Other companies that initially criticized our drastic measures eventually found they had to follow our example. While other companies were slashing their R&D budget, Infineon was relentless in seeking out cost-savings in other areas, preserving and ensuring our competitive advantage, and maintaining our high level of research and development at approximately 1 billion euro annually throughout the downturn cycle.

"As a follow-on program we launched Impact to strengthen our long-term competitiveness through further process improvements, best practice, and benchmarking, as well as transferring and outsourcing measures with a potential of another 500 million euro in savings.

"As a result of this contrarian strategy, Infineon maintained its strategic commitment to be a technology innovator and cost leader. One striking example for this is the successful development of the world's most advanced production technology on 300 mm wafers—which enables Infineon today to make the smallest chips on the biggest wafers for the lowest cost available anywhere in the world, more than one year ahead of the competition.

"Many armchair experts said 300 mm volume production couldn't be accomplished without huge investments. All of our competitors declined to pursue its development as aggressively as we did, given the tough economic times.

"But now 300 mm is a reality and a real industry benchmark, offering a strategic advantage to Infineon's customers, employees, and shareholders. After all, there are 2.5 times as many chips on 300 mm wafers as on 200 mm wafers, amounting to a cost advantage of more than 30 percent.

"By daring to think and act differently from our competitors, Infineon is well position indeed to profit first from the next market upturn while maintaining its technological pole position. Our success as a technology and cost leader would not have been possible without aggressive change-management, allowing Infineon to emerge strengthened from the worldwide downturn in the semiconductor market.

"I can only speak from my own experience, but I think the most important way to become a better leader is to have unshakable faith in your vision of the future. If you know your field well and are willing to run yourself and your organization hard enough, you can get ahead of what other people think is possible. Just like in auto racing—which is one of my hobbies—staying ahead of the competition is the essence of winning; whenever you lose commitment you've already lost the race.

"For example, increasing productivity while dramatically reducing overall spending in the middle of the worst downturn in semiconductor industry history was not only a tremendous challenge, especially when the downturn in 2001 with more than 30 percent was compounded by the unimaginable global impact of the terrorist attacks of September 11th.

"We endured a dramatic fall in D-RAM prices from $15 a chip in September 2000 to slightly above $1 a year later, and maintained our strategic investments into the future. We were motivated by our firm belief that there would be another market upturn, and we intended to be fully prepared for it, because at Infineon we understand that only technologically advanced companies will remain major players in our highly competitive industry.

"I've remained committed to my vision of Infineon as far more than being a cost-competitive chip manufacturer, branching deep our core competencies in the automotive electronics, communications, and memory semiconductor industries. Infineon is working to build on its position as a cutting-edge innovator, offering smart chip solutions that improve the quality of people's lives in ways they don't yet expect from a semiconductor company.

"That's why our patented products increasingly include innovations that are outside the realm of traditional semiconductors, with items like carbon-based nanotubes, neuro-chips, and new market applications such as smart textiles and e-farming.

"What sounds like science fiction is now science fact. Carbon-based nanotubes in particular promise to revolutionize the way we've been building semiconductors for the past 50-years by making it possible to integrate circuits naturally in patterns smaller than 100 nanometers, rather than etching them into silicon.

"This quantum leap forward will be matched on a more personal scale through the increased use of neuro-chips and bio-chips, which will be used to enable immediate and accurate disease identification, prediction of individual side effects, and predisposition for certain types of cancer. They will make medical diagnosis in hospitals not only far less costly, but much faster and more efficient.

"At Infineon, we are committed to creating a leadership culture based on a shared vision of our company five years down the road. We call it Agenda 5-to-1, because it communicates our commitment to focus within the next five years on becoming a top four global semiconductor player by achieving at least a top three position in each segment served, with a top two financial performance in all businesses compared to competition, and become the number one semiconductor company championing the solutions space.

"By directing our 30,000 employees worldwide toward a shared vision of our future, I believe Infineon will create an entrepreneurial culture of constant innovation and meet the future as a stronger company, a 21st century technology solutions provider with our best days ahead of us. Our company slogan, 'Never Stop Thinking,' very much reflects Infineon's competitive and creative mindset, which is the driving engine for our future success."

44

ANDRE L. LYNCH, CEO
Ingenium Corporation

If you don't leave room for people to risk and fail,
they won't achieve what you want them to achieve.

"No matter how upset a leader may be with anyone, that person should never leave the presence of that leader without their dignity intact. This requires that leaders always consider the impact of their tongues on the lives of others," says Ingenium's Andre Lynch.

"Individuals learn through constructive criticism, a sense that the leader has a long-term interest in the success of their lives, and, even if disciplined or terminated, that they are not devalued in the eyes of others. If you don't leave room for your people to risk and fail, they won't grow, and they won't achieve the results you want them to achieve.

"The key attributes of a successful leader are character, competency, flexibility, and empathy. The true measure of a leader is how he or she responds when the heat is on. Performance under pressure is the ultimate test of character.

"In business, my role is to service our employees, board, and customers. I live to serve them. The only effective way to become a better leader is through mentorship of a seasoned, disciplined executive who understands leadership through giving and serving."

45

DAVID A. STEINBERG, CEO

InPhonic

Listen to people and make them feel like part of a team.

"One of the most powerful leadership techniques that I've learned over the course of my career is to listen to people and make them feel like part of a team. Far too often, companies make employees feel like a cog in a larger machine and do not use the wealth of experience and knowledge they have under their own roof to develop innovative new business techniques and ideas.

"Early in building InPhonic, it was such a small team that it was important to solicit ideas and feedback from the entire staff in order to strengthen the business and identify new opportunities. This also helped to build an open culture of shared ideas and ownership in which everyone was welcome to participate.

"It led to some early innovations in the business model and the development of a strong corporate culture that empowered people to participate. One-on-one face time with employees and the ability to listen gives me feedback and perspective on the company that I otherwise would not see day to day from the office of the CEO.

"As a busy executive, it is difficult sometimes to make time for everyone. One of the ways that I do this is by holding a meeting every week with a different group within the company. This scheduled time gives me a chance to sit down and talk with employees and go through some things that are going on specific to their groups and get some valuable feedback on different initiatives or challenges. It is also an opportunity to brainstorm new ideas for different parts of the organization that I no longer manage directly, as we've grown into a larger company. This time helps everyone to feel like their voices are heard and gives me an opportunity to keep in touch with the employees on a regular basis.

"Reserving face time with employees is important, but just as critical is honing your listening skills to make the most of those increasingly precious opportunities. The key to effective listening is ensuring that when you speak with someone, that person has your total focus. This means being careful not to look at e-mail, pagers, and other devices. In fact, it often makes sense to speak with someone in a conference room or someplace outside your office to avoid these typical distractions.

"Another invaluable leadership tool is mentorship—from top to bottom throughout an organization. Not only do effective leaders mentor their key people, but they also continue to learn from their mentors, no matter how successful they've been. I've been able to draw immeasurably from the experience of John Sculley, who in addition to being InPhonic's first outside investor, a board member, and now vice chairman of the company, has been extremely generous with his time and has mentored me in every sense of the term. His experiences in business, as well as in life, have given me invaluable perspective.

"I suggest creating a formal mentoring program within the company that allows managers to meet one-on-one from time to time with higher level executives to bounce ideas off them and get advice. This does not have to be an executive that the manager works with on a regular basis. In fact, it's probably better if it's not, because that person can then provide more objective advice.

"If yours is a smaller company and there is a shortage of senior executives, managers should take it upon themselves to establish a relationship with someone in their local business community that can advise them on general business manners. This knowledge from an established business practitioner can be invaluable to a manager."

46

RICHARD A. GOLDSTEIN, CHAIRMAN AND CEO

International Flavors and Fragrances, Inc. (IFF)

*Give people the ability and authority to get things done,
and hold them accountable for the results.*

Richard Goldstein of International Flavors and Fragrances says that his most powerful leadership secret is empowerment, "giving people the ability and authority to get things done, and then holding them accountable for the results.

"If the person you want to empower refuses to 'take the reins,' then you have the wrong person in the position. Replace him or her.

"It is important to keep in mind that empowering someone does *not* mean that you allow them to act in a vacuum. People who are empowered to do their jobs must also know when to seek the counsel of others.

"How do you know when to consult with others? It's simple. If the decision you are about to take is reversible, or if the cost—financial or otherwise—of a potential mistake is affordable, then I say go for it. If, on the other hand, the decision is irreversible and the cost of a potential error is considerable, then it is probably prudent to consult with others first.

Richard offers this example: "Shortly after becoming Chairman and CEO of IFF, we took two significant and virtually simultaneous actions. First, we decided to reorganize our company, bringing our previously separate flavors and fragrances businesses together and implementing a global matrix structure to ensure the entire company was working toward the same goals. And second, we decided to acquire Bush Boake Allen (BBA), a half billion dollar leader in the flavor and fragrance industry.

"It goes without saying that I could not single-handedly manage the reorganization and integration, particularly given the exceedingly high and often skeptical expectations of the financial community. To help run our new matrix organization, I appointed a global head of business development and a global head of operations, and I named the former CEO of BBA to lead the integration.

"We were all in general agreement as to the overall course of action needed, and all three consulted with me on the broad issues throughout the transition. Nonetheless, there were instances when they took different decisions than I would have taken on particular issues. But leadership requires that the boss lets that happen.

"Why integrate flavors and fragrances? The answer is quite simple, though the execution of it was anything but.

"The consumer who wears our customers' fine fragrance is the same consumer who cleans her house with our customers' cleaning products. She is also the same consumer who eats our customers' snacks, brushes her teeth with their toothpaste, and drinks their beverages. We supply ingredients for all of these products. This holds true whether the consumer is in Singapore, Shanghai, Sao Paolo, or San Francisco.

"We reorganized because consumers consume our flavors *and* our fragrances, and because our customers manufacture foods, home and personal care products, *and* fine fragrances using our flavor *and* fragrance ingredients.

"What's more, many foods have both flavor and fragrance notes. And more and more fragrances are derived from or inspired by fruits, vegetables, herbs, and spices.

"In addition, our customers wanted us to be easier to do business with, and that included providing a single point of contact for all of our interactions, be they global, regional or local—flavors, fragrances, or both. They needed us to be able to go to market as one. So we did.

"What did we gain by integrating flavors and fragrances from an operations and marketing point of view? From an efficiency standpoint, there were compelling arguments to join forces.

"Why, for example, should we have two separate market research groups? Or two separate sales forces, for that matter? If a global customer has a need for both flavors and fragrances, why send two sales teams? Isn't that overkill? At the very least, by operating separately, we were missing a lot of opportunities for cross-category synergies.

"Our new structure and organization helped us address many of the critical issues we faced. First, our reorganization made us stronger, more flexible, and more efficient. The new IFF is better structured to serve our important global customers and to allow us to deliver improved customer service overall.

"Our new structure also has enabled us to go to market as 'One IFF,' which our customers told us they wanted and needed. Finally, as a result of the reorganization, we can better leverage our existing capabilities and, at the same time, find significant cost savings and supply chain efficiencies through the consolidation of our facilities, and improved asset utilization.

"By every key measure, the integration and reorganization have been successful. We closed a total of 26 facilities, and initiated, tracked, and completed 650 integration and reorganization-related projects.

"In terms of pure financials, we are meeting or exceeding our targets. We forecasted $70 million dollars in synergies from the integration. Our savings run rate today is over $80 million dollars. And when we announced our reorganization plans, we said we expected to yield $25 to $30 million dollars in annual savings by 2003. As of today, we are on track to deliver just that. The reaction from the financial community was positive.

"Overall the acquisition has been very successful. I am pleased to count IFF in the minority on that score."

How to become a better leader? "Learn to delegate," says Richard. "Stand back and give your reports the breathing room they need to take command and do their jobs as they see fit.

"Unless you believe the consequences will be too serious to bear, you should by and large accept the decisions your people take, even if they are not the ones you would have taken yourself. Impress upon your entire organization that, above all else, when faced with a decision—just do the right thing."

47

CHARLES FEGHALI, CEO

Interstate Resources, Inc.

Push to get things done.

"I am a practical person and spend more time on results that on analysis," says Charles Feghali of Interstate Resources. "Therefore my contribution here will be more a practical tip than a big secret.

"Many books have been written on this subject and many recipes and theories have been used by all kinds of people. Leadership is not only for the CEOs. Many people at any level in an organization or at any place in society can and do exhibit leadership traits. The technique or trait I describe here can be applied at any level in an organization, not just by CEOs.

"I would not consider what I offer here as a secret, and I do not know if I am one of the most successful CEOs. But I am glad to share with you here what I consider to be actually part of my everyday MO (modus operandi).

"A technique I found useful in my role as leader is to push to get things done, with the word *push* being the key. When I ask people to work on something, I always make sure they understand my expectations (the content of their work), and the reason I need it and what I am going to do with it.

"I then make sure we set a completion date. And if I do not receive it on the due date, they certainly hear from me! Some of those completion dates are driven by myself, but most are set by my people.

"I have come to realize and accept that most of my work schedule depends on the work that my people complete for me. That is why it is very important to know the completion date of the work I expect to receive.

"I see my role in this process as an orchestra conductor; all have the knowledge to do what they are supposed to do, and all know when they have to do it. When it all comes together, the results are a coherent, useful, and enjoyable piece of music.

"Some other traits and skills that come to mind when one pursues this technique include ownership, accountability, delivery, a make-it-happen attitude, and teamwork.

"If people ask for things but do not set a completion date, procrastination and delays occur. Then we are out of sync, and things don't get done.

"The sum total cannot be complete unless all the parts are ready. Otherwise, when the curtain is lifted, we all rush to complete what we have to do. A rushed job does not usually deliver the best results. Why settle for other than the best?

"As I said before, this is my MO and I put this technique in practice every day. It is not a one-off deal. It is ongoing. The examples are in everything I do, such as preparing for a board meeting, preparing for a performance review, assessing an investment.

"I do not believe there is a recipe to become a better leader. Still, one can practice—which is how one can learn—some skills that leaders exhibit.

"There are many types of leadership. To become a better leader, you first have to want to be one and believe you can be one. You have to work on it every day. When you acquire leadership skills, you exhibit them all the time. You have to. You cannot enter this arena as a temp. You join this group to stay there, because you belong there.

"Once you choose the type of leader you want to be, you should learn more about that individual, read his or her biography if available. Then start emulating him or her by applying some techniques that leader has used."

48

HOWARD R. CONANT, CEO

Interstate Steel

Maintain a high level of integrity.

Howard Conant suggests that the two most important leadership techniques are thinking outside the box and maintaining the highest level of integrity.

"When foreign steel was shipped all the way to Chicago, there were frequent insurance claims for damage where rough seas and inadequate packaging caused sea water to enter holds of vessels and damage cargo. While many of our competitors would submit claims that were artificially increased, anticipating compromise settlements, our claims were for precisely what we thought the damage to be.

"After our integrity was established and adjusters determined that our claims were fair, word got around that we could be trusted. The time spent settling claims was reduced to almost nothing, allowing both insurance adjusters and us to utilize time more advantageously.

"While I was chairman of Interstate Steel Company, in about 1985 we called on Hirsh Manufacturing Company, a manufacturer of steel shelving that recently had been doing a fairly large volume of sales for a small company—perhaps $40 or $50 million—but with extremely modest earnings, close to break even. Their credit lines were very limited from other steel suppliers because of their inadequate working capital and mediocre profits.

"The executives operating the company were straight shooters. I got good vibes when I met them. Our idea was to transform their steel buying from buying odd lots from distributors to supplying prepainted coils ordered to their precise specifications.

"I was so confident that this revised buying would improve their efficiency and reduce costs enormously that we set up a $2 million credit limit with a backup supply of another $2 million. It proved out and they became a $20 million annual account, with payments consistently on time. Since our competitors would not extend more than about $50,000 or so credit, this move was really out of the box. It worked.

"A person can become a better leader by honoring integrity. Succumbing to short-term temptations is likely to produce short-run gains, but long term, more severe negative results.

"Out-of-the-box thinking can be developed by examining traditional methods, or tradition itself, for validity. Encourage thinking creatively, even if some solutions at first sound goofy."

As a final thought, Howard offers these words from Socrates: 'The unexamined life is not worth living.'

49

ALEXANDRA LEBENTHAL, CEO
Lebenthal & Associates

Be a hands-on executive.

Alexandra Lebenthal describes herself as a hands-on executive because, "I ultimately believe that a company and its leader have a greater loyalty to its employees than the employees have toward them. Being involved as a result of employee regard means active participation in a number of small issues.

"To some, this may smack of micromanagement. Micromanagers override the ability of their employees and are controlling to a fault. While they may succeed, they do so without regard to the talent that exists in an organization. My style, in contrast, appreciates the talents of the employees and gives active assistance to reaching their goals and therefore the company's success.

"In the span of a few short weeks in the fall of 2001 our employees saw their world outside their window change by witnessing 9/11 across the street, and saw their world change inside when I announced the sale of our 76-year-old family business. Because of the commitment I have always felt toward our employees, and wanting to be an example for them, I called every employee in the days after 9/11.

"After our sale, I spent time walking around the sales floor and then meeting with every employee who would be let go after the deal closed. For those that remained, I was an active leader in the integration, even if some of the details were not one that a CEO normally focused on. Being aware of how change would affect them was my biggest focus.

"There is always an opportunity to become a better leader by treating every challenge or crisis as an opportunity to recognize when it's about to happen again. It not only makes you become stronger but also usually means that there was something good that came out of the first problem.

"I think everyone understood that, as a family business, there were a lot of complex issues that sort of went above them. I was tremendously involved; met with people personally. One woman who had been a clerk for twenty years, along with her sister-in-law, ended up crying in my office telling me how nice I was. I checked in with people on their job search, and still do. I sent the resumes of a few people to people I knew that could help them. Regarding the integration, I advocated for people and issues, probably at my expense.

"Bear in mind also that September 11 had just occurred and everyone here was feeling the effects of that. I wanted to be as supportive as possible. The night before we were all to return to work, I set up a conference call for the entire firm, and was clear in stating that, while we would be back, if anyone could not attend for emotional reasons, that was okay.

"I also set up counseling in the office and made sure that if there were people I knew who needed it but wouldn't go on their own, that their colleagues urged them to go. I didn't want them to feel that they had to because I was the boss.

"Two days after we came back, there was an announcement that they were going to do some dynamiting of the walls that were still standing. I told everyone that if they wanted to go home to miss it they could. As time went, some had a hard time, and I still had one-on-one conversations with them, and at that point gently urged that they needed to think about whether they could work down here at all.

"My advantage has always been that I put more pressure on myself than anyone else would, but I think as a family member I've always assumed a caretaker role with all our employees. I think they've felt that. I think it's also been a burden for me to have 100 other 'children' to watch over. I did have a hard time with this after the sale because I knew I was ultimately saying there is a limit to this relationship."

50

ROGER S. BERKOWITZ, CEO
Legal Sea Foods, Inc.

Listen to those around you and implement the best of what's suggested.

"Some years ago, I instituted a program called PAC, meaning President's Advisory Council. I hold quarterly meetings with randomly selected hourly employees who volunteer for the opportunity," explains Roger Berkowitz of Legal Sea Foods.

"PAC meetings let me talk directly and informally to those employees who have the most direct contact with customers. At Legal, this means wait staff, host staff, cooks, and bartenders.

"I hold PAC meetings without any management present, and I encourage the participants to 'cut loose' with their ideas and suggestions. Having over 50 enthusiastic, unencumbered employees at my disposal is an incredible opportunity in terms of gaining valuable feedback and applying necessary focus to important operational issues.

"PAC results have allowed me to eliminate chronic and universal issues with regard to service and menu. As an example, we eliminated surcharges on some vegetables and side dishes, because staff saw this as a guest annoyance. Based on staff experience and insight, we revamped much of our training to be more comprehensive and better targeted to particular problems.

"I tell them that we are here to brainstorm and to come up with the ideas and solutions. Oftentimes we debate their ideas in the forum. The best ideas that make it through the meeting are presented at the upper management meeting for discussion. If an idea is not implemented, I'll report back to them at the next meeting as to why.

"The fact that their ideas have been discussed, whether implemented or not, is generally appreciated by all and at this point has not proven to be unmotivating.

"Here's another example of how PAC information solved a specific problem. Over the years, the most popular dish Legal serves is the beloved stuffed shrimp. Unfortunately, we also receive more complaints about that item as well! It has always been a challenge to get our guests to agree on a preferred flavor profile for the stuffing.

"Well, during one of our PAC meetings, a member asked me a loaded question: 'What's the feedback on our crab cakes?' 'Fantastic,' I responded. 'Why?'

"'Well,' the person shot back, 'if you just modify the crab cake recipe to work on the baked stuffed shrimp, it might solve your problem.' Brilliant, absolutely brilliant. Twenty years of complaints evaporated overnight."

Yet another example: "I wanted to develop a program on ethics. Rather than just solicit feedback from my VPs and directors, I got my PAC members involved as well. The program has just been implemented, and I have complete buy-in from the entire organization because *everyone* helped to create it.

"PAC members serve for four meetings per year and have proven to be the cheerleaders of the organization. Morale has soared throughout the whole company, because every employee realizes he or she does have a voice, and each opinion can make a difference.

"In an industry severely hampered by the downturn in convention and business travel, we were able to focus more on local guests and have succeeded in making them more loyal. Guest complaints have been substantially reduced and compliments are up.

"We are seeing revenue increases despite being in a recession. I see a direct correlation between our success and PAC. Some of it becomes apparent in short-term results. The rest will become apparent as part of our long-term strategy. As an example: how our culture translates in the lowering of attrition.

"You learn to be a better leader by learning to be a better listener. Too many leaders feel obliged to always come up with the right answer unsolicited. The reality is, no leader has a monopoly on good ideas. Listen to those around you and implement the best of what's suggested. That's a formula that works."

51

CHARLES AYRES, CEO

Lehman Brothers Merchant Banking

*Mutual understanding and agreement of both boundaries and
consequences lead to truly superior execution of any vision or strategy.*

Charles Ayres also views himself as a very hands-on manager. "I like
to walk the 'plant floor' on a regular basis and interact at all levels," he
says. "I want the team to feel that I am around and care about each one
of them.

"I have a very open-door policy and basically say shame on you if
you have an issue and you don't seek me out. I try to make our employees comfortable that, although I am not the complaint department and
have no monopoly on good ideas, I do have time to listen to legitimate
ways to improve things.

"I also give people room to develop and decide on what becomes
their own style. I don't want anyone to be a pale imitation of anyone else.
Therefore, I give people room within the parameters of specific goals
that need to be accomplished. This allows people to get from stated A
to my expressed point B in their own way, where I am very tolerant to
their own individual style.

"Although as stated above, I am flexible on style, I try to be very
clear and regimented on structure, especially concerning who is playing
what role. I don't leave this to chance, and try to make sure that everyone is very clear about the role they are playing and what my expectations are. The more time I spend on this clarity up front, the more time
I save later, with better outcomes.

"Believe it or not, all the teams I have built and worked with, where
I was expected to play the lead, embraced the idea that I would be the

'Benevolent Dictator' when it came to caring for the culture of the group. Once the rules were clearly articulated and understood, team members took solace that I, not they, would have to enforce these rules—and that the rules would be the same for everyone.

"This is where trust and respect is crucial. If trust and respect exists for the leader, and the team believes that the leader-dictator (sounds dramatic purposefully) is inherently fair, then the team wants the leader to enforce, dictatorially, the established and agreed-upon rules. The team will continue to support and respect the leader until the leader no longer lives up to his dictatorial stature and is no longer evenhanded.

"In reviewing my most powerful leadership techniques, it is important to note that I am defining *leadership* as getting a group or team to do what you want them to do. Whether they admit it or not, adults in the workforce, even at very senior levels, like and need clear boundaries.

"My leadership secret lies in the clear communication of these boundaries, backed up with consequences if the boundaries are breached. I have found that mutual understanding and agreement of both the boundaries and consequences up front lead to truly superior execution of any vision or strategy.

"By just having the conversation, it naturally establishes credibility, control, and care. It focuses the group on execution of the task at hand, eliminates noise and distractions without squelching creativity, gives people confidence that the rules are the same for everyone with no special treatment for any individual, and allows for a fair, quick, and clear move on the consequences if the boundaries are compromised.

"Setting boundaries and consequences becomes self-policing, so that it saves the leader and the team time, since everyone is clear on what to do and how to act. It does, however, require the leader to live up to the responsibility of making good on both the boundaries and consequences that have been established and agreed upon.

"I have used this technique twice very effectively in leadership positions I have held in the past four years. Once as Head of North American Merchant Banking for Deutsche Bank and once as Global Head of Merchant Banking for Lehman Brothers.

"In both cases, within the first week of my appointment to the new position, I sat down individually, for at least an hour with each member of the group I was to manage. After getting to know them, I told them I wanted to be clear on my expectation for them and my managerial structure and style.

"I told them that I believed in a partnership model for investing, which revolves around a consensus-building process where the group as a whole would become comfortable or not with a potential invest-ment. I took them through the specifics of a deal decision process that would result in making or declining an investment that involved all of the partners.

"I then shared with them that from a cultural standpoint I would run the group as a benevolent dictatorship. I explained to them that to preserve the integrity of the deal decision process, I needed to create a safe environment in order to discuss potential transactions. This called for a culture that would allow for team members to feel that they could not only put the merits of a deal on the table, but also be comfortable discussing the warts of a transaction openly.

"To create this culture, I laid out the boundaries that would provide for and reinforce this supportive environment. I told them I would not tolerate anyone being mean-spirited, manipulative, divisive, or not a team player. This would be fairly determined by me and me alone, and the consequence was immediate termination. I told them that I would not let any one individual undermine what was best for the entire group, and that my responsibility was to the whole team.

"I then made sure that each individual clearly understood these boundaries and consequences and agreed to operate within them. If they could not or would not, I let them know that I would provide for a smooth transition over time, which would be preferable to agreeing to something they could not or would not be willing to live up to.

"In both of my experiences thus far, I have had great success with this model both in reducing turnover, making prudent investments, and building a sustainable organization. In addition, I have not had to move on the consequences and terminate anyone in either of these situations.

"Leaders are not only born leaders, but it helps! There is a certain genetic make-up that makes it easier to lead, including physical presence (not just size) and charisma. However, leadership skills can be learned, but must be stylistically consistent and comfortable to an individual to be accretive.

"The best way to become a leader is first and foremost to want to lead people. There are plenty of people who may think they want to lead but who really don't!

"Assuming this is not the case, becoming a better leader is an ap-prenticeship business. Having a mentor and being around many leader-ship models is key.

"Drawing the best parts of many leadership models that seem to resonate and work for you is a good start. Be the guinea pig yourself to determine what is effective. Weave these behaviors into your own style and try them out.

"However, you need to have conviction in your own model to be effective and improve. People have a sense if you are unsure of yourself and will not be willing followers.

"People want to be led by someone strong; who they believe will take them to the place they want to go. Understand this early and you will immediately be better at it."

52

LEO A. DALY III, FAIA, RIBA, CHAIRMAN AND PRESIDENT

LEO A DALY Architecture, Planning, Engineering, Interior Design

Positive interdependence.

My most powerful leadership technique," says Leo Daly, "is commitment to a concept that my firm refers to as *positive interdependence.*

"At LEO A DALY, we utilize positive interdependence as a driver for collaboration between project team members to ensure that we achieve the best possible outcome for each project and each client. To us, positive interdependence means that everyone involved in a project, or in achieving a goal, is vested in its successful outcome.

"This concept is an important part of my leadership vision. Its genesis was in a management strategy adopted by my grandfather when he started the firm in 1915.

"He successfully integrated architects, planners, engineers, and interior and landscape designers into teams to approach each project from a holistic, or fully integrated, approach. Although this approach is standard practice today, in 1915 it was quite radical.

"As a firm we take care to hire design professionals who are skilled team players. We then foster a culture of shared values based on professional respect. We encourage active discussion and input from our design professionals while exploring the firm's approach to a project. However, once a decision is made, everyone is expected to collaborate to achieve the goal.

"As architects, engineers, planners, and interior designers, we are always responsible for the performance standards of a vast number of consultants and subconsultants who actively participate in every project.

This challenge is magnified by the complexity of the projects that our firm undertakes and by the fact that we now employ 1,000 design professionals in sixteen offices worldwide. We use positive interdependence to streamline the design and construction process, and find that it also provides an effective means of problem solving.

"We begin implementing positive interdependence in the early stages of each new project. By integrating the activities of all the necessary players at every stage of the project, we can quickly establish aligned goals and objectives, clearly define expectations, fine-tune attitudes and values, and establish a total commitment to schedule and budget. The results lead to a high level of client satisfaction, which we use to our strategic advantage as a business development tool.

"Our means of establishing this commitment to positive interdependence varies from project to project. It is, however, deeply rooted in our corporate culture and influences our selection of consultants and subconsultants for each project. We then utilize whatever communications tools are necessary to sustain the high level of collaboration, communication, and trust necessary to achieve the maximum results on highly complex projects.

"While the technique of positive interdependence may seem an obvious solution, it is in fact very difficult to achieve. My grandfather and the founder of the firm, Leo A. Daly, Sr., introduced this process when he began integrating teams of architects, engineers, planners, and interior designers to collaborate on projects. Since that time, positive interdependence has evolved at LEO A DALY to include all members of the team, from the design concept stage through to construction administration.

"One of the best recent examples of positive interdependence in our firm is the design, engineering, and construction of the new headquarters for First National Bank in Omaha, Nebraska. LEO A DALY was selected as the design architect from a shortlist of six international architects.

"After reviewing several locations, our client decided to build a new signature tower and complex in downtown Omaha. The design of this project was intended to both create a new corporate image for the First National Bank and to create a catalyst for the development of Omaha's downtown.

"We selected an extraordinary group of professionals to work on this project and to design a state-of-the-art tower and complex that accommodated our client's diverse needs. The design team was based in our Washington, DC, office while the engineers, project managers, and interior designers were based in our domestic headquarters in Omaha.

"By utilizing positive interdependence as a tool, we used the collective intelligence of all members of the team to design the project. This process also allowed us to deal with potential design challenges efficiently and effectively.

"We also established a formalized strategic alliance partnership with the client and the contractor, Kiewit Construction, to ensure that the project was built to the highest possible standards while also keeping on time and on budget. The strategic alliance process also allowed us to take advantage of composite construction practices to reduce cost. These savings were reinvested back into the materials and workmanship of the building.

"What made this strategic alliance succeed was that the client was intimately involved at every stage and, therefore, actively participated in problem solving. With a project the size and complexity of a corporate headquarters, there are usually a percentage of errors and omissions calculated into the agreement. The client's active participation and oversight, together with the constant dialogue between the architect, LEO A DALY, the general contractor, Kiewit Construction, and the subconsultants, kept the errors and omissions to a minimum.

"The client's active involvement in the strategic alliance partnership also led to both transparency in decision making and a sense of trust among the key players. As a result, when a major problem did occur, there was an immediate response among the players and very little finger pointing.

"For example, midway through the project the custom curtain wall manufacturer went into bankruptcy protection, which could have led to both finger pointing and costly construction delays. Because the selection of this manufacturer was a joint decision made by the strategic alliance partners, and also because it was based on the manufacturer's qualifications and the best information available at the time, there was no finger pointing.

"Once the partnership became aware of the problem, the partners spent their time dealing with the solution rather than blaming each other. The result was a joint effort to retrieve the custom components from the first curtain wall manufacturer and integrating them into the design of the replacement manufacturer.

"Safety in the workplace was also an extremely high priority for this project. The close collaboration established between all parties by the strategic alliance partnership led to the team receiving the STAR award from OSHA for excellent standards in workplace safety. The injury rate on the job-site was 61 percent below the national average, which is quite an accomplishment with an average of 450 workers on the site everyday.

"The result of the integration of positive interdependence and strategic alliance partnering is an elegant, award-winning tower and headquarters complex which has established a design benchmark for downtown Omaha, and has prompted the investment of over $2 billion dollars in the downtown area. LEO A DALY is also very proud to have First National Bank as a happy and satisfied client.

"Surround yourself with the best people, listen to their advice, and empower them to succeed. Establish the person's challenge and then provide him or her with manp1ower and technical resources needed to succeed (within reasonable budgetary guidelines.) And, probably more importantly, give that person your trust and reinforce that trust publicly in front of his or her peers and other employees."

53

GUERRINO DE LUCA, CEO
Logitech

A sense of humility is the antidote for complacency.

Logitech's Guerrino De Luca considers himself an apprentice. "I may be the CEO of a billion dollar company," he says, "but I know that I don't have all the answers. I will always be an apprentice, always trying to learn and understand more, surrounding myself with the brightest people I can find, and always staying grounded. I believe this apprentice frame of mind is critical to success, whether you are the CEO of Logitech or a manager of a local restaurant.

"I'm never comfortable setting myself apart from everyone else. If you carry a title like CEO to heart, you'll view the organization through polarized lenses, only seeing what you want to see—not what needs to be seen.

"Maintaining an apprentice's perspective keeps me on the same plain as other decision makers in your organization, creating a healthy team dynamic. As an apprentice, I have the opportunity to glean from the expertise of my management team and let others around me become more comfortable leading. My vision is the accumulation of the 5,000 pairs of eyes that comprise Logitech.

"As a CEO, a leader, and an apprentice, I never tire of fresh thinking. I relish it. I crave it. And I try to surround myself with those who challenge me. We're a global company with an internationally diverse team of empowered people. Our senior executive team includes a Frenchman, an Italian, a Taiwanese, a Dutchman, an American woman, and two American men. I encourage everyone to think like a CEO, a

CFO, a COO. Some of the best decisions I ever made were the decisions made by others.

"The apprentice also has a sense of humility that is an antidote for complacency. You can never think that you've done it all, that you've reached the pinnacle of your profession just because you carry a title like CEO. A complacent leader is the foundation for a house of cards that will inevitably come tumbling down.

"One might say the apprentice's approach is similar to Zen's *beginner's mind*. While I'm not formally educated or practiced in Zen, I believe it's critical to always maintain an open mind, to be a knowledge sponge, surrounding yourself with the brightest people and willing to soak up their thinking.

"As a CEO, I have to be a generalist, and allow my specialists to develop expertise in their areas. It's important for me to have an open mind in order to truly hear them, and to be able to act on the knowledge and insight they present to me.

"For example, shortly after I joined Logitech in 1998, we were gearing up to launch our first cordless desktop—a keyboard-and-mouse combination. The value was clear to many: provide a complete cordless solution for consumers who were craving the opportunity to clean up their desktop and free themselves from cords.

"It wasn't immediately clear to me. I'd always been of the opinion that consumers were looking to buy components individually. I felt there were consumers who wanted mice, and those who wanted keyboards, but very few of those who wanted both. Ultimately, in the role of apprentice, I let our seasoned product management team continue with the process and launch the product.

"It's a good thing. Ever since, our cordless desktop products have been among our bestselling products. With the cordless desktop as a major factor, we've now sold more than 40 million cordless devices, and Logitech is recognized as the world's leader in cordless peripherals.

"One might argue that staying with the apprentice mindset might lead to the perception of weakness. I would argue that failing to take the apprentice mindset would lead to danger. With the apprentice frame of mind, I understand that I need to gather as much information as possible from my key sources to make good decisions.

"Without the right information, a leader could either suffer from indecision, or worse, make bad decisions. And, clearly, making bad decisions is the most basic way to ruin your credibility.

"One example of how the apprentice mindset led me to the correct decision came in early 2001, when we acquired Labtec, a manufacturer of peripherals that were complementary to our own product offerings. By all accounts—unlike the vast majority of acquisitions—it's been a very successful merger. But initially, I wasn't so sure about it. I looked at the business and the products, and I wasn't convinced of the value of the asset on paper.

"Shortly before the deal was struck, we had a meeting with some key members of their leadership team. When I met their team and listened to them articulate their vision, my impression changed dramatically. The soft value of the acquisition—the human value—was tremendous.

"As an apprentice, I'm able to gain collective knowledge and experience from our new colleagues. In many acquisitions—often failures—the acquired companies are forced to conform to the parents' ways. In this case, we saw the value of Labtec's engineering, processes, and leadership. Not only have the pieces been successfully integrated, Labtec has helped redefine and enhance the Logitech culture. And it was a success only because of the Labtec people.

"I won't ever make an acquisition or transaction without understanding the people. I could fall in love with a business that might not look as good on paper but has good people. And I might avoid an opportunity that is a hot deal if it doesn't have the people that could help define the Logitech of the future—and help further my apprenticeship. "It also helps, as CEO, to have the hands-in-the-dirt experience that gives you more credibility. People sometimes ask if, at Logitech, I have to be a techie for some of our techie employees to respect me. Having started in this business as an engineer, a technologist, I may have more credibility with our engineering teams and our product marketers. Understanding how all of the proverbial cogs and gears work together is as important in my role as understanding my responsibility to our investors as a public company.

"Fundamentally, Logitech is and always will be a product company. And, as CEO, I have to be the ultimate marketer both to my internal team and to external audiences. I've always believed that some of the best technology marketers are engineers by trade.

"A good leader is also a good communicator. An apprentice asks the right questions and knows how to listen. Logitech is an interface company—we make products that are the touch points to connect humankind and the digital world. As a management team, we understand that how we interface with each other shapes our vision and determines how successful we will be in creating great products.

"Part of being a good communicator and a good leader is acting in a manner consistent with what's communicated. As a CEO, I preach. As an apprentice, I practice. As a leader, I practice what I preach. I hold myself accountable and I expect accountability from those around me.

"As a CEO or an executive of any kind, one is never done learning. I watch the different people around me to see how they lead, and to see how I can learn from them. I'm absolutely obsessed by sucking in their good traits and rejecting the bad ones.

"In my career, I've had good bosses and bad bosses. And I've learned a lot from both. I've watched how *not* to do things from the bad bosses. The key is to maintain a high level of intellectual honesty and skepticism. I never discount anything entirely, and at the same time, I try not to drink the Kool-Aid when everything seems rosy. With that kind of skeptical mindset there is so much that can be learned every day.

"Finally, I believe a key trait for successful leaders is their ability to detect their environment and to apply their brain, their experience, and their personality to that specific context. Success and failure will be determined by how they meld with their surroundings. Successful leaders have the innate ability to perceive their environment and the needs of all of those entrenched alongside of them. That's because they are always listening, and always learning. Just like an apprentice."

54

C. JAMES JENSEN, CEO
Mara Gateway Associates
People make decisions based on feelings, not facts.

For Jim Jensen of Mara Gateway, the most underutilized asset in negotiations is the human element. "Write this down," he says, "and commit it to memory: *People make decisions based on feelings, not facts.*

"This statement is the antithesis of most teachings about the 'Art of the Deal.' And, I am not suggesting for a moment that you ignore or dismiss the facts. But if you want to elevate your effectiveness as a negotiator—a key attribute of a strong leader—find some common ground or a way to bond with the person with whom you are negotiating. In the case of competitive negotiations where other individuals or parties are competing with you for what you are attempting to achieve a personal relationship with the person you are negotiating with will give you a competitive edge.

"If people like you and want to do business with you, they will make every effort to effect the transaction with you over your competitors. Expect the evening call at your home where the person with whom you are negotiating may suggest some ideas as to how you might restructure your offer to insure you the greatest chance of succeeding your negotiation.

"I want to share a real life negotiation where going out of my way to meet the people I was hoping to do business with resulted in successful conclusions that I believe would not have happened had I not made the effort to meet with these people in person.

"In April 2001, we were negotiating to purchase a Holiday Inn property in Santa Clara, California. We had a third party negotiating on our behalf. On Friday, April 27, the negotiations broke down. On Monday, April 30, one of our partners and I flew from San Francisco to meet with the sellers in San Clemente.

"We met from 10:00 AM to 5:00 PM It was a long day. There was a lot of giving and taking. We got the deal done fairly to both sides. Although the deal points were very important to both of us, it was the sidebar conversations about our kids, little league, the San Diego Padres, Chicago Cubs, Michigan State Spartans, Washington Huskies, fraternities, etc., that made real people treat each other as real people.

"The meeting had begun on an adversarial tone. But by remaining centered and nonconfrontational, focusing on interests, not positions, and genuinely attempting to understand the other side's objectives, we were able to sort through the issues, reduce each other's resistance, and have a successful meeting. Our parting words at the elevator were the promise to have a fun dinner together in the near future.

"The next day I received a fax at my home from the principal negotiator of the seller we had met with. The fax read, 'Thanks again for coming down yesterday. It's the only way to really get things done.'

"People have feelings. By nature, they really want to be loving and helpful. Most want win-win outcomes. Nothing can accelerate this probability more than face-to-face meetings with the people you are doing business with, provided you are committed to creating a meaningful relationship."

55

DAVID B. SNOW, JR., PRESIDENT, CHAIRMAN, AND CEO

Medco Health Solutions

Identify the noble cause that will drive the business as well as the hearts and minds of the company's employees.

"An effective CEO integrates multiple techniques to lead an organization," says David Snow of Medco. "The most successful leader will first identify and then clearly articulate the *noble cause* that will drive the business, as well as the hearts and minds of the company's employees.

"By definition, the noble cause is a view from inside the company looking out—not about a self-interest, but rather revolving around a selfless intent to help others. Those pursuing a noble cause inherently believe that if they always do what's right for others, their reward will follow.

"Every business—whether it yearns to cure cancer or build a better mousetrap—can discover its unique noble cause. The noble cause becomes the underpinning of what it does; it sharpens the vision, directs the strategy and guides the tactics. In turn, that noble cause places the enterprise on a critical path of integrity that embodies how you conduct your business.

"The noble cause creates an alignment that unites your corporate goals with your customer's objectives. Of equal importance, the noble cause serves as a catalyst to stimulate the passion required for your people to dedicate their hearts and their heads—and willingly make the sacrifices required—to achieve world-class performance.

"While many tasks of a corporation require teamwork, teams don't determine the noble cause. It's the single point of accountability and the sole responsibility of the company's leader, charting the course for what will ultimately become a CEO's lasting leadership legacy.

"At Medco Health Solutions, our noble cause is to continually improve a system that provides millions of Americans with access to the world's highest quality pharmaceutical health care, and to ensure that care is affordable for our clients, who bear the cost. It has been my experience that finding the noble cause within a company drives a passion for world-class excellence, which, in turn, drives growth and profitability.

"Through the process of defining and articulating the noble cause, your organization is essentially developing its brandable difference—the characteristics that leverage your unique strengths, drive demand, and make your products and services strategically relevant to your clients and customers, which forges long-term loyalties and enduring success.

"Fresh out of grad school, I started my career by running hospitals. It didn't take long to realize that even in the best health care system in the world, there was significant opportunity for improvement. This kindled a passion for reforming the medical delivery system, preserving those things that worked well and fixing those things that didn't. It's a focus that I've carried with me whether I was starting a business, managing a business, or taking a company public.

"In 1988, with three partners, I founded MHS—Managed Health Care Systems, Inc., which established Medicaid HMOs in several states. It was founded out of a desire to extend managed care to benefit the underserved—those who didn't have access to the health care system.

"We built the company as a vehicle to provide better health care for the poor, while at the same time reducing costs for taxpayers. It created sanity out of the insanity that defined the health care system for the underserved—how could you not become passionate about that?

"That noble cause channeled my passion into a vision and strategy that drove a business plan to recruit the believers and win over regulators and legislators whose cooperation was essential in delivering on the promise. MHS continued to thrive well after I moved on to my next venture and, known today as AmeriChoice, it is part of United Healthcare.

"The noble cause is also a means to restore lost glory. When I agreed to take on the President and COO role at Empire BlueCross BlueShield, it was a turnaround situation.

"What had at one time been the premiere health care company in New York, had eroded into a financially struggling organization with a damaged brand, no membership growth, and disheartened employees. Although the company said that its goal was providing high-quality health care for its members, its actions said otherwise.

"The company was inwardly focused and its members became disenfranchised. Even seemingly simple execution, such as member communications explaining benefits and coverage, was mired in corporatespeak that resulted in confusion, drove up inbound complaints, and yielded high rates of rejected claims.

"The turnaround hinged on a noble cause. We needed to reclaim our rightful place as the pre-eminent insurer in New York, to be the best again in the minds of our customers.

"That was the start of a four-year journey to achieve world-class service through operational excellence. The vision was articulated across the organization and employees who yearned for something in which they could again believe were transformed into a passionate and proud army committed to their clients in order to rebuild their brand. It redefined the culture. The noble cause stirred a passion that led to performance and profits.

"We transitioned from negative growth to a quarter of a million net new customers a year, the strongest growth rate in twenty years. We improved our margins and our bond ratings. Empire BlueCross BlueShield grew to attain revenue of more than $5 billion and became a stable and profitable health plan that we took public late in 2002 under their new name of WellChoice.

"Communicating clearly and effectively is a linchpin to building the alignment around the noble cause. The most effective leaders articulate in a simple and straightforward manner what they are doing and why, which results in a natural alignment of interests. Great institutions are built with believers and volunteers, not mercenaries and conscripts.

"The best leaders surround themselves with diversity in the broadest sense. A diverse management team of individuals who challenge convention and bring to the table multiple perspectives and experiences have 360-degree vision—no blind spots. It's the only way to reach the best result every time. If each member of the team is a clone, you haven't protected your company from your blind spots.

"Hire the right people who can execute around the vision and the passion—the noble cause. You can't do it all by yourself.

"Never forget that you get the best out of people by igniting their passion. Those people are motivated by a burning internal desire to achieve greatness, not because they're getting paid a few extra bucks. They won't check their hearts and heads at the door. And they won't abandon you in times of adversity."

56

JOHN E. RAU, CEO
Miami Corporation

Communicate the high expectation that everyone should think strategically about what is best for the company.

"I like to ask people to answer questions as if they were sitting in the CEO's chair. This seems to have several useful results," says John Rau of Miami Corporation.

"It communicates the high expectation that everyone should think strategically and about what is best for the company. And people usually live up to whatever expectations you have of them.

"It gets people thinking outside their own area or function, and this often generates empathy for their colleagues in sister divisions or functions when you are asked to look at these relationships 'from above.'

"Even before officially starting as CEO of Chicago Title and Trust Company, I gave the senior executive team an assignment to 'write the *Business Week* article from five years in the future that explained what killed the company.' It forced them to take the CEO's perspective on the real threats to the business as it existed and accept that material changes were essential.

"In doing goal setting, I will ask the manager to write a performance review of himself or herself, giving the best possible rating and listing the achievements that led to that rating. This helps get some real focus on what excellent results really look like.

"This is a never-ending challenge—like improving your golf game—and there are similarities in how you do that.

"Watch the best and let the *image* of what they do sink in. Read a lot of case histories in books and current periodicals, and rethink how you would have dealt with the issues and whether other outcomes were possible so you can simulate strategic thinking in a broad variety.

"Keep yourself open to feedback on your own impact on people. Ask them to imagine they are the CEO and ask how they would decide if being CEO was their job.

"People vary. Some will give you parochial or self-interested answers and some will shift their perspective. It is the process that matters, not the answers.

"How do you get honest feedback versus people who just want to butter up the boss? You get more by giving more. It is true that, unless you set an example of being candid and of allowing constructive criticism to be given safely, all you will get is what people think you want."

57

ATWOOD COLLINS, III, PRESIDENT

MidAtlantic Division, M&T Bank

Focus fueled by a passion, and commitment to consistently apply it.

"I wish the ingredients for successful leadership could be boiled down to a step-by-step recipe. It is more complex than that," says Atwood Collins of M&T Bank. "Nevertheless, I have found a few techniques, which consistently applied, have yielded successful results.

"The principal technique I use is focus fueled by a passion, and commitment to consistently apply it. What do I mean by focus? Focus first on what objectives you want to accomplish, what your organization is good at, and how you are going to do it.

"For example, in our business of banking, there are approximately 9,213 competitors all doing the same thing: taking deposits and lending money. But the incredible thing is they do it with wildly different results. What does that tell you? Success lies in the execution, not the strategy.

"Successful banks, and M&T is among the best, focus on doing 'the common uncommonly well.' Give the client what is expected and do it consistently. Sounds simple, but it is incredibly hard. Hard in the sense that consistent execution requires tremendous attention to detail, significant energy to repetitiously execute, and a commitment to be tireless in the pursuit of being consistent. So, to boil it all down a few simple steps.

- Focus on what you want to achieve, and how you are going to do it.
- Develop simple metrics to reassure your success in achieving those goals you have established. I stress *simple* metrics, because

a lot of businesses try to measure everything, which in reality is measuring nothing.
- Be consistent in how you execute the objectives.
- Relentlessly review your performance and adjust or retool where necessary.

"I have two examples in our business of how we applied what I have just discussed. One of our first acquisitions in the late '80s was a mutual savings bank. This was a significant undertaking at the time, because we were roughly the same size, and the acquired company lacked the staff and infrastructure to do what we, as a successful commercial bank, knew how to do.

"The first thing we did was focus on what the company did successfully. In dong so, we found out that they had a long history of lending on commercial real estate, primarily multifamily. They not only had an excellent track record measured in terms of charge-offs as a percentage of loans outstanding, but also they had a staff who knew how to do it, and a servicing infrastructure that could successfully monitor it.

"In terms of executing what they were good at, one of the first things we noticed was that they had a mortgage committee made up of primarily outside directors. The key ingredient was a centralized focus of decision making with consistent execution in applying it. This was somewhat unusual in that directors rarely get involved in day-to-day decision making.

"However, New York City real estate is so unique that local specialized knowledge is key to being successful. We made the chair of the committee one of our directors who was a successful New York City owner of multifamily and commercial properties. We then recruited other owners and developers as directors.

"They met every week and reviewed with management all loan requests. The insight that they brought to the table was invaluable. In many cases, they owned a similar building in the neighborhood, and we could focus on the underlying operating metrics of a particular property with an objectivity that would otherwise be missing.

"The committee also provided us with an appropriate check and balance in our decision making, as bankers sometimes make the mistake of 'never meeting a loan they didn't like.' As a consequence, I believe our mortgage committee and the directors who serve on it have been critical to our success in this business over the last fifteen years. Again, the key leadership ingredient is ability to focus and measure key operating economics of a commercial property with objectivity.

"Another example of an application of what I have been talking about involves our efforts to systematically and constantly measure the activities of our bankers. We developed a simple system called Sales Force Automation (SFA) at a cost of a little over $1 million. We built it as opposed to buying someone else's version of what they thought we should measure.

"While SFA performs numerous functions, in its most basic form it measures three activities:

1. Calling activity on prospects and customers
2. The resultant loan and fee pipeline and the percentage of likely success
3. The booked outstandings or fee based transactions

"Simple metrics, which consistently applied, create a tremendous sales management tool.

"At our monthly and quarterly review meetings, in addition to reviewing the financials, we have each manager review these simple sales metrics for each business. It is amazing to see the linkage between the calling effort, the loan pipeline, and the resulting impact on our balance sheet and income statement. Once again, these are simple metrics, consistently applied."

As for becoming a successful leader, Atwood says, "there are certain things that can be taught and others are acquired through trial by experience. However, I would again first start with a focus on what you want to accomplish and how you are gong to do it. I'm not talking about a mission statement. What I mean is specific objectives with detailed means and dates by which they will be accomplished.

"Remember, as a famous architect once said, 'Life is in the details.' Share your vision plan with your employees and organize their activities around accomplishing the objectives. Listen to and encourage their participation in the plan to achieve these objectives. Set up consistent simple metrics by which you can gauge how you are doing.

"As a leader you can have all the vision you like, but really it is not your vision that is important, it is the one that your people can see. People see a vision of the future when they can clearly connect their objectives and their goals to the value that you are trying to create.

"Your first job as a leader is to help them to make that connection. Then you need to create consistent simple metrics by which you can gauge how you and your people are doing. And finally, not only do you need to be passionate in pursuing your goals, but you have to really love your customers.

"All of this takes huge amounts of focus, passion, and commitment, as well as bucket loads of energy and ownership and accountability. That is why there are far fewer leaders than managers.

"Finally, be relentless in your passion for consistently pursuing your goals. Many managers constantly underestimate the amount and level of energy it takes to do the common uncommonly well."

58

JUDITH HARRISON BODE, FORMER CEO

Monet

Build a team that is able to meet new challenges.

"Why do some companies exhibit continuous growth and others do not survive?" asks Judy Harrison Bode. "The difference, I believe, is that the organization that recognizes that success is only the beginning is the organization that will thrive. As a leader you must build a team that is prepared and able to meet the new challenges that come with success.

"It is your responsibility as a leader to choose the right people. Mold them into an effective unit and sufficiently train them to use their individual strengths in the service of the team, and they can adapt to the environment—success will follow success.

"The foundation of a superior organization is a shared vision and a shared commitment. In each of my organizational incarnations, my first task was to make certain that everyone knew our goals and participated in formulating the path we would take to reach them.

"Each team member knew his or her part in the organization and how that function meshed with every other function. They committed themselves and their staffs to the success of the enterprise as a whole, knowing that if one element failed, the entire effort would fail.

"Communication mechanisms were put into place to effectively air and resolve organizational conflicts.

"Key to success was the organization's ability to recognize and believe that continuous growth required change. Sustaining growth requires an organization with the capacity and willingness to identify and react to a dynamic environment.

"Charles Darwin wrote more than a century ago that survival depends not on size or strength, but on the ability to adapt. It is a principal, not only of biology, but also of commerce, that any organism that fails to respond to a changing landscape is doomed to extinction.

"The organization's ability to respond in a unified manner to a dynamic environment has determined the level of achievement that the company has attained.

"I am credited with revitalizing and growing two dominant accessory businesses, The Monet Group and Liz Claiborne Handbags. Both companies were the market leader in their respective industries, costume jewelry and handbags. Both companies had lost their luster and were experiencing rapid decline of sales and profits.

"The reason for their decline was that neither company could change to react to a dynamic market. Consumer preferences were changing, the customer was commanding increased control over the channel, company operations were inefficient, new manufacturing competencies had to be developed, priorities needed to shift. Speed to market, maintenance of quality, and the importance of new product introductions were critical elements of success.

"It was easier to ignore the results rather than fix the core business. Management could continue to claim that they were the market leader and blame others for the weakening of the company. The goals and business priorities were not clear to the organization. Organizational conflicts prevailed.

"Functional areas put out fires, but there was no unified company effort. There was a lack of acknowledgement that past success was only a beginning, and that the company must adapt to the changing market for continued growth.

"Being new, I explained my situation to the team. I needed their help to understand key issues, business drivers, and the organization. I conveyed my first thoughts: that the team was responsible for our company's success, and the company is a great one, but performance in recent years has not been acceptable. Going forward, we would build on past success, make all changes necessary to maximize value, and always act with a sense of urgency.

"Before we took any significant actions, my first task was to quickly gain a shared vision and a shared commitment. The management group undertaking a fact-based business assessment of the company and market accomplished this.

"Were we functionally excellent? How did we measure against key performance indicators? What were appropriate matrices to measure our success against? Were we communicating effectively with our customers? Were our selling strategies achieving our goals and our customers' needs?

"The answers came back from the group. Our customers believed that we were too large to ignore, our allowance contributions artificially supported our funding, but our lack of innovation did not warrant continued investment. We learned that we must innovate to deliver value to the consumer and customer leadership faster than our competitors.

"The next step was to ensure that the team was comprised of the right players. Being the right player meant that you were technically competent and had the ability to work across all functional lines. Initial success reinforced to the team members that commitment to the company winning over their own functional interests paid off.

"Once we had the right players, governed the company objectively, and based our decisions on facts and customer/consumer demand, we began to see results. Cost of goods dropped; sales and margins increased.

"Our customers, and the retailers, invested in the business based on our innovation and leadership. We regained and increased our 'share of wallet.'

"A *Forbes* reporter wrote: 'Strolling through the Monet showroom recently, this reporter could see the results. Trifari has regained its youthful, trendy look. Marvella's once cheap-looking faux pearls have new sophistication. Capitalizing on nostalgia, Monet has reintroduced a line of lovely jewelry, using its original 1940s designs.'

"A bigger compliment came from a past president of Monet who said, 'This product was what I was trying to achieve but could never get design, sales, and manufacturing to work together on.'

"In ten months, the company became profitable once more. Customer sales increased by 12 percent, despite a declining marketplace.

"The same performance happened at Liz Claiborne. Within two years, sales increased by 42 percent, pretax earnings by 116 percent.

"Lessons learned? Success is only the beginning. A team must be prepared and able to meet new challenges. It was once said about Monet, 'Harrison has cut a diamond from the rough, but she can't admire it for too long. Costume jewelry is an unforgiving business. And while a diamond does not shatter, a glass one will.'

"A former colleague defined an effective leader as someone who organized people and resources to achieve a goal. A good leader can communicate in writing and verbally. He or she can gain commitment and make a believer out of you. Delegate, but know when to stop. A leader is self-confident and cares about the development of people."

"I believe that these traits define a leader. Each individual must assess their own strengths and honestly recognize their shortcomings. The key is to understand the characteristics of good business leadership, be honest about your needs, and take action."

59

GARY E. COSTLEY, CEO
International Multifoods
Values are the foundation of all great leaders.

Gary Costley of Multifoods believes in values-based leadership. "I am convinced that people will follow a leader they trust, and trust is built by actions, not words," he says. "To be successful, chief executive officers need to lead by example and model the behaviors and attitudes they expect of their employees.

"Values are the foundation of all great leaders. People will not follow someone who they don't view as credible and who hasn't earned their respect. I try very hard to communicate what the values of the organization are, and then live those values as a role model for the organization. People respect that and, as a result, are more likely to go the extra mile to get the results.

"At Multifoods, we found ourselves in a unique situation in November 2001, having just acquired the Pillsbury Desserts and Specialty Products business, which served as the basis for strategically refocusing the company on branded foods. We had a new leadership team that included people from a variety of consumer packaged-foods companies. One of the first steps we took as a new leadership group was to agree on the values we would adhere to—and model—for our employees. We built our 'brand' new company's foundation on personal integrity and high ethical standards, a focus on partnership and teamwork, a passion to win, and the drive to deliver outstanding performance. In the past several years, we have worked hard to ensure that our actions as a leadership team are consistent with these values.

"Before joining Multifoods, I served for two years as dean of the Babcock Graduate School of Management at Wake Forest University. In this role, I led the faculty and staff through a process to define the school's vision, mission, and values. Through this process, we agreed that our overriding purpose was to be excellent in both teaching and the advancement of business knowledge through leading-edge research. To ensure that we stayed true to the school's mission and values, we subsequently put in place a reward system grounded in three key principles: teaching, research, and service.

"Despite never having been in a leadership role in academia, the leadership skills that I developed during nearly 25 years at the Kellogg Company seemed to be just as important at Wake Forest. That's because they are values based.

"Becoming a more effective leader takes work. Leaders are developed, not born. Leadership, like all other interpersonal skills, requires consistent effort. The job of a leader is to get everyone aligned around a shared set of values and pulling in the same direction.

"Those values then become the guideposts for the organization. While that sounds difficult, it isn't. For example, at Multifoods, we started with some simple, fundamental rules of engagement: tell the truth, treat people with respect, listen, do what you say you are going to do, help other people get things done, and hold ourselves and each other accountable for agreed-upon results.

"I believe that if leaders and organizations start with these types of standards as a base, it is possible to get most people to sign on to the effort. For those who do not agree with the values, they can vote with their feet and leave.

"At the same time, once the organization agrees to a set of values, leaders need to hold people accountable and ensure that everyone in the organization lives those values. For example, if personal integrity and ethical standards are a core value, leaders must not tolerate unethical behavior in the organization.

"Living the values that are agreed on is critical to being a successful leader. Imagine how much more effective organizations would be if their leaders listened, treated people with respect, told the truth no matter how difficult, and held themselves accountable for results. Many of the corporate scandals of the past several years would never have come to pass. Values-based leadership is the right answer for corporate leaders today."

60

MARC MAURER, PRESIDENT

National Federation of the Blind (NFB)

Articulate and demonstrate an empowering philosophy.

"As president of the National Federation of the Blind, the largest membership organization of blind persons in this country," says Marc Maurer, "my most effective leadership technique is best described as the articulation of an empowering philosophy of blindness, and then demonstration of this through both conventional and unconventional means.

"I speak frequently and write even more often about the NFB's philosophy on blindness, which challenges the traditional attitudes toward the blind. This belief system offers to those of us who are blind and visually impaired an understanding of ourselves as normal people with the characteristic of being blind. We understand that blind people with proper training and opportunity can do any job commensurate with their aptitudes and talents.

"Blind people can live full and complete lives, including raising families, being adventuresome, participating actively in local communities, and doing whatever they desire.

"The second and probably most important aspect of my leadership technique is that I find opportunities to demonstrate this empowering philosophy by doing things not usually associated with being blind.

"I build large charcoal fires and grill steaks for blind and sighted alike, I split wood because at one time I didn't think a blind person could do that, I lead groups of young blind persons through the construction site of our new Research and Training Institute, and I teach other blind persons how to use a chainsaw.

"During leadership seminars that I conduct with members of the NFB from around the country, I demonstrate this philosophy through group examination of dilemmas presented in letters I have received from blind persons. I ask those attending the leadership seminar to consider questions posed in these letters.

"Using our understanding that the real problems of blindness are the attitudes and misconceptions held by the public, and blind people ourselves, rather than simply the fact that we can't see, I guide the group through a process of self-exploration. I use a Socratic questioning style, which encourages those participating to think pragmatically about the real problems of blindness, and, through this questioning method, I demonstrate that I expect a lot from them.

"Frequently blind individuals, no matter if they have been blind all their lives or are new to vision loss, are regarded by those around them as not able to do much. I try to counter that by demonstrating to them that they are worth my time and energy and that I expect excellence from them. The most elegant gift you can give individuals being groomed to be leaders is the expectation that they will use their talents and abilities fully.

"I believe my leadership style is built on a commitment to a vision that I learned from previous leaders of the organized blind movement. This vision demands that a leader of this proud minority group lead by example.

"Integrity is something that is demonstrated and not simply talked about. My leadership continues to foster a culture of disciplined action built upon a tradition of compassion for each other and a dedication to an uncompromising belief in the inherent potential of blind people."

61

SY STERNBERG, CHAIRMAN AND CEO
New York Life

Don't outsource your strategic thinking.

"Simply put, we don't outsource our strategic thinking," states New York Life's CEO, Sy Sternberg. "This might sound strange, but you would be surprised at how many companies have become dependent on external advisors, consultants, and researchers for much of their strategic decision making.

"Consultation and research can help you test your hunches and sharpen your thinking, but you can't let those tools serve as a proxy for leadership.

"I encourage everyone on our team to think independently and to resist becoming intellectually captive to the pronouncements of 'experts' or to the latest trends within the industry. In our business, it seems as though there is always someone eager to convince you that you must abandon your business model and adopt theirs. During the dot-com days, the experts were telling us that selling life insurance through agents was a thing of the past, and soon, all transactions would take place online.

"Had we listened to this advice, the results would have been disastrous. The fact is, we are not that easily blown off course. We have a strong culture. We have a clear understanding of our unique strengths. And most important of all, we know that leadership means doing your own thinking and going your own way.

"There have been several instances, in recent years, where New York Life has distinguished itself by not following the herd.

"In the late '90s, during the height of the bull market, many insurance companies rushed to demutualize. Like New York Life, these mutual companies were not publicly traded and had no shareholders. In mutual companies, policyholders, not stockowners, vote for board members and receive all dividends.

"Our newly demutualized competitors were able to structure stock deals to acquire other publicly owned insurance companies. But, in 1998, when we looked at New York Life's strong cash flow and our ample surplus, we concluded we had no need to issue stock to fund future growth.

"In a recent report on New York Life, the AM Best rating agency concurred: 'Sy Sternberg and his board found that their company already had what other companies coveted and hoped to achieve through demutualization: a powerful brand, a productive distribution system, strong capitalization and revenues.'

"But the bigger issue was my personal belief that there is an inherent conflict between managing a company for the needs of your policyholders versus the demands of shareholders. Investors tend to judge performance by how much you can maximize profits quarter-over-quarter or year-over-year. Policyholders, on the other hand, are looking for long-term security and stability 20 or 30 or 40 years into the future.

"The decision, for me, was absolutely clear: Our most important obligation is to serve the needs and respect the priorities of our policyholders.

"In the end, we gained some significant competitive advantages by maintaining our commitment to mutuality. We can still offer our customers *participating* (dividend-eligible) whole life, a product that continues to grow in popularity. More importantly, our mutuality lends us an important distinction: People know us as an insurance company whose every action is uniquely aligned with the interests of its policyholders.

"I also took what some might call a contrarian view on another recent trend in the industry: the move toward financial services consolidation. A few years ago, many of our competitors were busy reinventing themselves as financial services supermarkets, diversifying into banking and brokerages.

"All of the consultants and the brand experts were trying to tell me that our company was too narrowly focused. They even suggested we give some serious thought to changing the New York Life name, a move they claimed was necessary if we hoped to sell other, noninsurance products.

"My instinctive judgment said, 'Our name is our most powerful asset. Why would I jeopardize that?' Additionally, I had to conclude that, even in a mature market, there were enormous opportunities for growth in the life insurance business. First-year premiums for policies sold in the U.S. exceeded $11 billion annually. However, no single company had more than a 6 percent share of the U.S. life insurance market. In a fragmented market such as this, market share gains of just 2 or 3 percent will have an enormous impact on a company's sales revenues.

"This is exactly what took place at New York Life. At the end of 2000, New York Life's market share was about 4 percent. By 2002, we had *doubled* our sales by capturing another 3.4 percent of the market. When you couple this performance with our strong growth in emerging international markets, such as China and India, it is apparent that our narrow focus on life insurance is actually a strategy for rapid, robust growth.

"Certainly, we will continue to seek opportunities to market other financial products that are a good fit with our brand and our strengths. But rather than tinker with our identity, I think it would be far wiser to persuade consumers that the brand attributes of our life insurance business—financial strength, integrity, and humanity—are an integral part of everything else that we do.

"You move towards real leadership by becoming less dependent on others to do your strategic thinking for you. You move towards real leadership by demonstrating originality, independence, and confidence.

"How do you become a leader? The answer is simple: Learn to trust your own judgment. Learn to stand on your own two feet."

62

ROBERT P. BAIRD, JR., PRESIDENT AND CEO

Norelco Consumer Products, Philips
Domestic Appliances North America

Strategic probing.

"Much is taught and written about what we need to do as leaders. The *what* is energizing, whether it is changing culture, hiring and grooming talent, redefining the mission, or creating a new business model. But successful leadership is more about *how* we do what needs to be done," says Robert Baird, Jr., of Norelco Consumer Products.

"The technique I most frequently employ to get the results I want, regardless of the specific challenges I am confronting, is the practice of *strategic probing.*

"Strong executives are quick to formulate hypotheses, whether it is about strategy, executional recommendations, culture, or people. We get to where we are because we are smart and opinionated. Whether armed with concrete data or gut instincts—preferably both, most of us quickly figure out what we need to do and act quickly.

"What is often more difficult, however, is to identify the right team for the time and circumstances we face. Whether it is a strategic business or key people issue, strategic probing enables me to adjust or confirm my initial hypotheses. So I can better ensure that the right decisions are made, and that those decisions are energetically and skillfully executed and owned by the right people.

"Strategic probing of individuals can be uncomfortable, which is why it takes practice and great finesse. It is important to create an environment that respects the integrity of the person and is therefore conducive to dialogue—the free exchange of ideas and alternatives. The goal is to get to the best, not the *good enough*.

"When the technique worked most effectively, I did my homework, kept digging until I was satisfied we were at the level we needed to be, and ensured that the interaction ended on a positive note. While there is nothing sexy about this process, it is the critically important spadework that produces the best outcome.

"The steps in the strategic probing process include:

1. *Preparation.* Formulating hypotheses and communicating expectations.
2. *Creating a conducive climate for interaction.* Warm, friendly, humor and a little flattery helps relax people, so use it. Read your audience; respond to their body language.
3. *Posing the leading, open-ended questions.* Start easy, with positives. Later, begin heavier probing and challenging assumptions.
4. *Deepening the dialogue.*
5. *Peeling the onion.* Asking "why" (and "why not").
6. *Bringing the meeting to positive closure.*

"The result should be a deeper understanding of the persons rather than the personas; a revealing X ray of the problems, challenges, and opportunities; a robust set of alternative solutions, if appropriate; and a clear course of action that energizes the team. The process not only produces the best outcome for the organization, but also brings out the innate problem-solving creativity within people and raises their performance to a new level.

"I consciously practice strategic probing in interviews. Following this practice, I have been well able to separate the wheat from the chafe and those who claim versus those who excel at a competency. Also, this technique can be used to identify values, ethics, cultural fit, and the high-maintenance versus low-maintenance executives.

"During one interview with an ex-CEO, I kept probing to differentiate accomplishments from reality. Through this process it became evident that this person was unethical. He and his management team had essentially been cooking the books."

By way of further example, Robert says, "I joined Philips as the CEO of their Domestic Appliance Group for North America, in May of 2002. This division had been incredibly successful, delivering nearly a decade of runaway success, surpassing every operation plan objective.

"Yet, for the prior eighteen months, the core shaving business (Norelco) had been under siege. The organization was facing tough competition and did not have some of the critical competencies that would be needed to regain and sustain market leadership.

"Also, the organization had grown very comfortable, given that winning had been so easy, and had lost its competitive instincts. People throughout the organization had extensive years of service (average of twenty years), and had succumbed to the inevitable complacency that accompanies such long-term success. For those who have read *Good to Great*, by Jim Collins, you can really identify with this syndrome.

"My challenge was to magnify awareness of the new reality confronting us, while maintaining an environment that would be as conducive as possible to objective, nonthreatening interactions. I needed to be able to make the assessments necessary to put together the team that could turn things around and take us where we needed to go.

"My hypotheses included the likelihood that some of the team had so much invested in the past that they would be unable to make the paradigm shift to the new direction. Others in the organization were clearly able to adapt and blossom under the new direction.

"Through relentless strategic probing over the initial 90-day period in town meetings, team meetings, and one-on-ones, the critical business and people solutions became readily apparent. One member of the team was not up to the challenges we faced, another was reassigned to a position that was more compatible with his talents, and one individual was very underutilized and could be a catalyst for change.

"As a result of that process it also became evident that several required competencies were missing, and that a deeper cultural transformation was needed. The team was transformed over the year into a much more energized, hungry, and effective management team.

"Strategic probing also works very well during strategy sessions. An example arises at Philips during marketing plan meetings. Despite given clear direction that I wanted a focused discussion of key strategic choices we would be making, the team came forward with a ten-inch binder of data.

"After politely listening to PowerPoint presentations of data, I stopped the meeting to get up and lead a discussion on using strategic probing. During this dialog, we were able to peel back the onion and gain much greater insight into the key drivers (or lack thereof) of the business.

"The marketing team had been formulating pedestrian marketing plans, including TV commercials and displays to drive share. During the probing it became clear that we were targeting virtually all audiences with the same old marketing techniques.

"Also, our household penetration was eroding and our franchise was aging. Our core users, who are incredibly loyal, were not being creatively persuaded to trade up to our new products.

"Despite the dramatic evolution of electric shaving technology during the last decade, we were not breaking through to blade users. As a result of this 'velvet hammer' session with the team, we redefined our entire marketing plan to focus on increasing household penetration, accelerating our repurchase cycle among core users, and beginning youth recruitment initiatives.

"This was a fundamental shift that resulted in some amazingly innovative new approaches for achieving our strategies. To date, the business has responded and our share has rebounded. Importantly, the team has also learned a new technique to challenge themselves.

"Another subset was a product line for teens that the marketing group had developed. It was a good idea and the team was rushing against time to get it launched. When we met, we discussed all the good aspects of the proposal.

"But in their haste, they had not sufficiently thought about how this could potentially cannibalize the base business. The packaging was far too similar to our core line, did not have a unified look, and was lacking an intrusive subbrand. My strategic probing determined that several critical strategic issues had not been addressed.

"In spite of the deadline and their zeal to launch, I posed the key questions and engaged them in active dialogue. The team showed their disappointment, but as we engaged the issues more deeply, it became clear that what we had was only good enough, not the best.

"The team regrouped and brought forward a much better recommendation. In the end, the product line had a very successful launch and enabled us to more deeply penetrate this important target group with less threat of cannibalizing the base business. Everyone felt good about the end result.

"It is exceptionally helpful to have great leadership mentors. I adopt the best leadership techniques from them, and eliminate those that don't square with my personal values or preferred style. I also learn from the industry's thought leaders—people like Bennis, Covey, Bossidy, and Welch. Attending seminars, like the Center for Creative Leadership, also has good value.

"But the most critical leadership qualities require strong emotional intelligence, and the foundation of emotional intelligence is self-awareness. It is ironic that the closer we get to the top of the mountain, the less we get what we most need: feedback!

"I not only want to know how the company and the management team are doing, but how *I'm* doing, and what I need to be doing better. I measure that two ways: Am I creating the kind of culture that will optimize individual and group performance, and am I personally modeling the values and demonstrating the leadership that is needed.

"Because few people are skillful or courageous enough to give candid feedback to the boss, I ask for it anonymously. I then set improvement goals and hold myself accountable for achieving them. When necessary, I won't hesitate to use a professional coach.

"If I am not accountable for improving my leadership effectiveness, I can't expect it from others. Ultimately, I am trying to enable an environment where anonymity is no longer necessary—where multidirectional feedback is seen simply as a way of doing business."

63

PAUL I. KAROFSKY, EXECUTIVE DIRECTOR
Northeastern University Center for Family Business

Be adaptable.

"The attributes of leadership are situational," says Paul Karofsky, Executive Director of Northeastern University's Center for Family Business. "What works in one organization may be a cause of failure in another. Accordingly, adaptability is one of the most powerful leadership skills. The extent to which a leader can adapt his or her style, approach, and skill set to a situation or organization at hand is a great contributor of success.

"Adaptability does not require one to become a total chameleon. Hopefully one's values and personality endure. But style must adapt. We can take clues from others and modify our approaches to the situation at hand.

"Ambiguity might keep people up nights, but anyone seeking exquisite clarity and simplicity in his or her career ought to look for a non-leadership position. Leaders, by definition, have followers. Followers need direction. Direction requires decision making. Decision making requires consideration of options. And consideration of options involves dealing with ambiguity.

"Leaders learn to tolerate ambiguity on an ongoing basis through experience and effective decision-making processes, and by gathering good information to assist in the decision-making process. A paperweight that sits on my desk reads, 'No one can take the ultimate weight of decision making off your shoulders. But the more you know about how things really are, the lighter your burden will be.'

"Being used to running a family business in the wholesale distribution field, I made decisions as the need appeared. There is an added burden to being the son of the founder, and even more so for the grandson, since fewer than one out of three family businesses survive through a second generation, and fewer than one out of ten survive through a third generation.

"Non-family members in the company have performance expectations of the next generation of leaders, and so does Dad. Often, family members must meet entry criteria, determined at a family meeting, including attaining a certain level of education and outside work experience. Not allowing family members to enter the business simply because of their last name helps. So does clarity on roles and responsibilities, the assignment of a mentor, and routine performance appraisals.

"When involved in our industry's trade association, I learned to listen to others and hear not only what was said, but what was not said.

"I learned to speak last so I could digest the comments of others, respond more thoughtfully, and be better heard. I adapted to the needs of the situation. Though the end result and decision reached by the group might have been the very same one I was thinking of at the moment the problem was presented, by enduring and supporting the group process, everyone owned the solution and it was much easier to implement.

"You can become a better leader by first being a follower under both effective and ineffective leaders, by learning from experience, by learning to tolerate ambiguity, by delegating effectively, by believing in the capacity of others to grow, by being committed to a lifelong education for yourself and others, by standing on your own yet being interdependent, by understanding yourself, and by making use of a personal counselor, mentor, or coach."

64

KENT KRESA, CHAIRMAN AND CEO

Northrup Grumman Corp.

Work for those who work for you.

Northrup Grumman CEO Kent Kresa offers the following leadership tips:

- Management and processes are learned. Leadership is probably not.
- Work for those who work for you.
- Don't run your organization. Lead others who follow you, and have them run it.
- Save yourself for the big decisions. Most of the running of the organization will be done by your direct reports.
- Delegate authority and help your people develop themselves as decision makers.
- Never humiliate an opponent or other organization you take over.

65

MICHAEL D. DREXLER, CEO
Optimedia International

Always encourage your staff to stretch.

Optimedia's Michael Drexler advises, "Always encourage your staff to *stretch*. The norm is based on general goals we set as a percent increase year over year using economic indicators for our business classification. The stretch goals exceed the norm by a certain percentage based on estimated predictions of specific product categories.

"We have regular stretch goals that are high enough to raise our level of performance, yet reasonable enough to be achieved. And we are generous with rewards when they are met. Most of all, we share the spotlight so individual recognition is acknowledged by all.

"An individual we hired as an entry level professional was given research assignments to begin his career path. He began working alongside a senior strategist who was responsible for developing advertising media strategies for blue chip companies.

"While not specifically asked to create strategic platforms, he was asked to provide any points of view or opinions he might have about the data he was collecting. Pretty soon, he was not only developing data but including important insights about the information from which conclusions could be drawn.

"Praised and encouraged to do more and cited for his good work, in no time he became one of the most quotable researchers in the business, making speeches, serving on industry panels, and authoring reports. He now heads the research department of a major advertising media agency.

"There is a great difference between being a boss and being a leader. A leader inspires people to do more than they think they are capable of doing. A leader engenders team spirit and collaboration. A leader encourages prudent risk taking without severe penalty for occasional mistakes. In other words, he is a cheerleader, who also participates, guides, and always ensures a positive environment.

"A boss is someone who often dictates how things should be done. He gives the orders. Employees are expected to follow-through rather than initiate and innovate. Either they fit the mold or they're out. A leader asks people to break the mold."

66

ALBERTO ALEMAN ZUBIETA, ADMINISTRATOR
Panama Canal Authority (ACP)

Change constantly.

"The Panama Canal Authority is charged with the management, operation, maintenance, improvement and modernization of the Panama Canal. The ACP is independent and autonomous from the Government of Panama, functioning as a market-oriented model that focuses on customer service and reliability. This shift in business model has yielded substantial dividends to customers and world commerce, with the canal recently setting impressive safety and efficiency records," says Administrator Alberto Aleman Zubieta.

"It is essential to understand the real nature of your company and the products and services you provide. We live in a dynamic environment and therefore we have to change constantly. Knowing where your company is and where you want it to be in the near future are key elements for developing a strategic vision.

"There are three essential characteristics of a good leader. They are:

1. Having and implementing a vision and sense of direction to lead toward that set goal
2. Placing priorities
3. Empowering your people

"I believe that an organization's people are its lifeblood, and that leaders are only as good as the people who support them. Empowerment means letting people know they are valued, giving them autonomy and opportunities that will lead them to reach their highest potential. Having the best team of informed, knowledgeable, and trustworthy people is a crucial and indispensable element in achieving an organization's goals and a leader's vision.

"At the end of 1999, during the U.S. handover of the Panama Canal to the Republic of Panama, I assumed leadership of the ACP. Managing the historic Panama Canal is no small or easy task. Nevertheless, the challenge, and especially the honor, of taking the responsibility for Panama's national symbol of pride and patrimony, was truly exhilarating.

"Our vision for the canal is to bring an 89-year-old waterway to 21st century standards, and to steer the canal towards profitability and future viability so that we may meet the needs of our customers and guarantee dividends for the Panamanian people. Our goal is to make Panama the most important canter for transshipment and logistics of the Americas and to get the most benefit from our geographic position.

"The ACP has moved from a public utility, user-based operation to a market-oriented business enterprise to better meet the demands of our customers, thus requiring a cultural change in our organization.

"We are in the process of this cultural change and business model. We have worked with our management team and the canal's world-class workforce to develop the canal's vision, mission, and values, which are the bases that will support our strategy to achieve our vision. We have created an education program for our entire workforce so that they can understand the business we are in, the environment, our competition, and our goals, mission, and vision. These, together with a strong communication and information program, will help accelerate these required changes in our company.

"We also met and consulted with many of our customers to identify their needs. We implemented a new toll structure based on the market's needs. We also made capital investments by increasing and improving our equipment and machinery. In response to security developments, we expanded our security operations and installed new security systems.

"The ACP has already started to reap the fruits of this process. Our investments in training, equipment, and technology have helped achieve an impressive and new safety record.

"Since we assumed control of the canal, the ACP has steadily reduced the number of maritime accidents. We have also significantly reduced the time vessels take to travel the canal.

"This means that the canal route provides faster and more reliable shipment of goods for customers and consumers alike. The Panama Canal Maritime Operations Department, as well as the Human Resources

Department's Training and Development Division were awarded ISO 9001 certification, and the Environmental Management Division was awarded ISO 14001 certification. The ISO certifications corroborate the quality of service provided by the Panama Canal to its customers, and attests to its continued commitment to satisfy their needs and expectations.

"With a dynamic management team, and the ACP's highly qualified workers and employees, we have been working steadily toward the achievement of our collective vision for the canal. Together, we will make sure that the gains we have achieved will continue on in the coming years.

"All the above would not have been possible without the partnerships we have forged with people, and by empowering our work force to make informed decisions, to innovate, and to react to the requirements of our customers. The history of the Panama Canal is filled with great leaders who have been pivotal in enabling and building one of the engineering marvels of the world.

"Leadership is formulating decisions, overcoming mistakes, and innovating as you respond to the evolving needs of your clients. You do not inherit leadership. You have to earn that leadership and respect.

"There are those that believe that being in a position of command makes them a leader. There is nothing farther from the truth. People may obey because of fear or necessity. A true leader inspires the people to perform at utmost capacity rather than only obeying orders and acting on them.

"Leadership is both challenging and exciting. Lead and learn, learn and lead; these are important ingredients in becoming a better leader."

67

PATTY DEDOMINIC, CEO
PDQ Careers

Make new contacts and continue to cultivate the old.

Patty DeDominic's most powerful leadership technique is to make new contacts and continue to cultivate the old. "Remember that your network must be made up of diverse leaders from all walks of life. Speak only the truth. Give good input and feedback. Integrity does not have to always be loud, but it can never be silenced.

"My life has been enhanced by friends and colleagues who have helped me to get nominated to boards of directors, clients who felt we offered honorable service and recommended us to others. I once gave a (free) speech to help government managers hire extraordinary and cost-effective employees and consultants. A short time later I was given some business, less than a year later our firm received a $700,000 contract.

How does one learn to be a better leader? "Watch the best in action," says Patty. "Take extraordinary classes at schools and universities. I recently attended one at the Kennedy School of Government at Harvard: 'Leadership in the New World.' It was the best $5,000 investment I have made in over a decade.

"Also, practice. My years coming up through the ranks to eventually become chairman of the LA Area Chamber of Commerce (http://www.laacc.org) gave me good experience and plenty of great examples to follow. A few to avoid, also!

"Cultivating contacts takes time and energy. It takes a lifetime. It is a continuous process, particularly if one owns a business or is serious about growing their career.

"It is also like a garden—if you don't plant anything, you can't complain if all you have is weeds.

"It's amazing what we can now do with e-mail. I use Outlook, my Palm Pilot, and my cell phone to keep in touch with our key customers and the executives on the CEO's management teams.

"For me, since I am in human resources/staffing and executive search businesses, the biggest mistake I see people making is to get to know recruiters *after* they are looking for a job or when they are out of work.

"Job seekers often forget to tend to their networks before they need it. Think of it as a garden, and just know you are going to be hungry for something next spring, so you'd better do some good planting now.

"Another mistake is not bothering to follow up with people who referred you to good leads or who tried to help you. Sometimes people only connect with potential referral sources when they have a need. It is important to send good referrals out to the network, not just make withdrawals.

"When networking or running into people at functions, avoid monopolizing someone's time or telling stories that are way too long. Sometimes people can become clingy or take advantage of help offered by taking up hours of a mentor's time and not really giving anything back in return.

"To get to the point where others ask you to give speeches and serve on boards, become as close to an expert in something—your profession or your hobby—as you can. If you have no experience in these areas, try Toastmasters as it is a good place to get experience and tips in a supportive environment.

"If you want to serve on boards, get some experience with the nonprofit that you love. Many nonprofits are crying for volunteer leaders. There are many opportunities. Keep your eyes open and step forward next time you notice that something is missing or needed."

68

PAUL LABRIE, CEO
Pilotage

You can never own a customer.

When Paul LaBrie of Pilotage reflected to determine which best secret or technique to discuss, he focussed on the marketing/sales fallacy of, 'I *own* that customer!'

"Many marketing-sales types feel that they *own* the customer if they have a sale in progress or have sold something to them in the past.

"Marketing-sales is different in the field of OEM (original equipment manager) sales, but the same principles apply, especially when you have bona fide input, such as an existing customer from which to launch a product application search.

"I taught my company's marketing and sales people that you can never own a customer. They were shown how to scour the customer for more and more applications—being adamant about finding other existing applications that the customer has, as well as new applications that were coming up.

"No active company has *no* new applications. An active OEM customer who has no applications means that the salesperson covering the account has insufficient knowledge.

"The technique was in setting up a feedback system that made it obvious if salespeople were not following up on competitive applications, as well as new applications." Paul came to call the results of this system *customer applications reports,* or CARs. "This form, which grew in use because it worked, was a moving, continuously upgraded report.

After a while, these reports became instrumental in driving the manu-facturing requirements of my company.

"I remember two situations that sort of prove the case. One was with one of the company's best sales reps, Lee.

"We were in the San Jose area. I saw, from the CAR report, that one of our major computer manufacturers should be ready to place another yearly order for thousands of parts—a big order.

"Lee said that he knew the customer, the customer was in his pocket, and that he would tell me when a new order was to be placed. Not yielding, I had him call the customer.

"Lee found that a new buyer, not knowing my company had been providing these products, went to an alternate vendor whom he knew from his past employment. Lee went nearly ballistic—he had been neg-ligent.

The story ends well, however, when Lee "got the order changed to my company on the basis that the products were superior to the com-petition's. From that point on, Lee became such a believer in the CAR approach that he introduced it to his other OEM products.

"The second situation came from a trip to San Antonio where another of my great sales reps, Bob, was covering an ATM system man-ufacturer. Bob told me that there were no other applications for my products in this company. I told him it was impossible that this major manufacturer had no new applications going.

"I asked the customer's engineer if he would be so kind as to allow me a visit of his facilities. He was not only willing, but was proud to do so. During the tour, I found two other OEM applications where two other engineers, both of whom Bob did not know, had specified infe-rior competitive products.

"We did win back the customer for these two applications, but we lost time and had to work uphill in order to achieve success. Obviously, Bob also became a believer in CARs.

"With today's database systems, systemizing such an approach is easily done. But the system alone, without the conviction of the people at its helm, is insufficient to achieve the benefits that are available only through determination, perseverance, and service to the customer.

"The secret is to have a system that keeps informing you to follow up as to when and where the next golden plum will be coming along, without having to be solely reliant on others."

69

PETER A. BENOLIEL, CEO (RETIRED)

Quaker Chemical Corporation

*Integrity, honesty in dealing with people, and
openness to relationships and ideas have served me well.*

"I am flattered that you would wish to include me in this book," says
Peter Benoliel, "but I am not sure I am a candidate, as I retired as CEO
of Quaker Chemical Corporation back in 1991—over ten years ago. As
Reginald Jones, former CEO of General Electric, so aptly put it, 'I've
gone from Who's Who to who's he?'

"Actually, I don't think there are real secrets regarding leadership.
It comes in every sex, every color, every nationality, every religious per-
suasion, and manifold leadership styles.

"My experience as a naval officer was by far my best practical preparation for leadership. Integrity, honesty in dealing with people, and
openness to relationships and ideas have served me well. People knew
that they could count on my word, and that I would do what I promised
to do.

"As to giving you examples of the above, I would have to say that it
was in everything I did, every day I was the CEO of Quaker Chemical
Corporation. I felt I had responsibilities to the stakeholders in the company—namely, our shareholders, our employees, our customers, our
suppliers, and the communities in which we operated.

"I realized that I could not optimize returns to any one stakeholder
without compromising the others, so the challenge was to provide opportunities and returns to each group in a balanced manner. I made it
clear to all shareholders, either by letter or in personal contact, that this

was my approach to the management and leadership of Quaker Chemical Corporation.

"How can a person learn to become a better leader? Principally, in two ways: By emulating people who have inspired them either in real life, history, or fiction. And by reading and studying leaders of the past, the present, and fictional. I would suggest a reading list that included the Bible, Homer, Plato, the Greek playwrights, Thucydides, Plutarch, Shakespeare, Thomas Hardy, Joseph Conrad, and biographies of great men, especially Abraham Lincoln and Gandhi.

"The above is not all-inclusive, but hopefully suggestive. I can assure you that my lifetime of reading and studying was the best instruction for leadership."

70

LEN ROBERTS, CHAIRMAN AND CEO

Radioshack Corporation

Passion, vision, and trust.

"I've watched and learned from people's behavior at every level of an organization, not just senior management. And I've observed behaviors that can be learned and practiced to achieve higher standard of excellence," says Len Roberts of RadioShack.

"One of the first things I learned was that leadership qualities go far and above so-called command and control issues—giving out orders and expecting people to follow blindly. That's a recipe for disaster.

"I think there are three qualities that distinguish a good leader: passion, vision, and trust.

"Passionate people get things done. Passion for doing what you're called to do informs every fiber of a true leader. Passion shows. Passionate people energize other people and build enthusiasm. And let me tell you, enthusiasm is contagious.

"Here's what I mean: In March 2003, RadioShack celebrated its tenth annual national sales meeting. We call it Peak of Performance. I started this tradition when I first joined the company in 1993.

"Well, one of our big sales winners got up on stage to accept his trophy, and he said that enthusiasm was his key to success. He said, the more you give it away, the more you have. I love that. It's so true.

"When people become enthusiastic and passionate about what they do, they create their own chemistry and throw off as much enthusiasm and passion as they make. And the lines between business and personal, or school and personal, become so blurred, they become one. And at that point, it's hard to say whether someone's working or whether they're playing, because they're having so much fun.

"Leadership behavior number two is vision. To have vision means to be gifted with an aspiration, a picture in the mind's eye of what we want to be. Vision is all about integrating new knowledge with old to create better methods, techniques, and ideas to accomplish goals.

"Developing that vision is all about having the ability to listen as well, because vision can't be developed in a vacuum. It takes input from throughout an organization.

"When I got to RadioShack in 1993, they were calling themselves 'America's Technology Store.' Only problem was, the public didn't buy it. Consumers looked to RadioShack not for computers or the latest technology, but for the things they couldn't get anywhere else: the cables to hook up their stereo to their TV, or specialty batteries, or electronic parts. They were looking to RadioShack for solutions for their problems.

"So before I even took the job, I went into the field and talked to store managers and salespeople. And I listened. What I learned was that the public also looked to us for friendly, knowledgeable help.

"We learned who we were from listening—and from that, came the vision, which is to become the most powerful one-stop shop to connect people to the wonders of modern technology. We put that vision into the brand proposition we still have today: 'You've got questions. We've got answers.'

"To fulfill our vision, we lined up all our strengths to become more than just a store, more than a nationwide chain of stores. We became a *retail services concept,* unique in our industry, dedicated to solutions for our customers. Our company's mission became simply to demystify technology in every neighborhood in America.

"Being a retail services concept is all about our assets of 35,000 knowledgeable team members in 7,200 stores, all in the service of our customers. Our brand position is an unquestionable strength, too. Everyone knows it and associates it with us. This valuable consumer perception is no less than our core identity—and a core competency.

"So, listening to your people, listening to learn, to encourage, to help them grow—then helping them formulate a vision of how they can get where they want to go—is essential to outstanding leadership. Vision comes from listening ad learning.

"The next element of leadership, number three, is trust. Trust is a *must!* In our organization, everyone starts out with a large measure of trust. It's just like a bank balance. Each person has a credit of trust they can draw upon.

"I trust that our people will deliver on their commitments, do what they say they'll do, when they say they'll do it. When a manager tells me he'll have a report to me on store sales in the southwest by Friday, he's made a commitment. He has a responsibility. I expect that he'll have the figures to me by Friday.

"Now, if something comes up—a family emergency—and he can't get me the numbers, all he has to do is let me know, 'Hey, Len, I won't have the numbers by Friday.' That's fine. I can adjust. I can deal with it.

"What I *can't* deal with is this: He doesn't deliver the numbers, doesn't call me, doesn't tell me why he's late, or what's going on. I've made commitments based on his commitment to me. If he doesn't come through, I can't, either. I've just lost a measure of trust in that person. The balance on his 'trust account' has just been debited.

"On the other side of the coin, the leader has to earn the employee's trust, too. You have to be consistent in your feedback processes, in how you manage individuals. And most important, you have to always tell the truth.

"If we as leaders expect to build trust in those we lead, we have to earn it by demonstrating that we can be trusted to have their best interests at heart, and tell the truth.

"Truth sometimes hurts. It's hard to tell someone they're not performing to expectations. But leaving them in the dark—or telling them little white lies that they're doing well when they're really not—is worse.

"People want to know where they stand. I believe people want to do an outstanding job. Therefore, being level with someone and telling them the truth, even if it's a hard truth, is best for everyone. When honesty and mutual respect prevail, the foundation for trust is built on solid rock.

"During my first days at RadioShack, I was asked to make a few comments to management, since I was the new kid on the block. I was also asked to keep those comments brief, since management would be in shock that a person like me, from the fast-food industry, was now head of a technology-oriented retailer.

"But I chose to make an immediate impact, instead of wasting time. So I got up and talked about organizational change, and about how change was worrisome, but that I though people were ready for a change, to make things better. I said that the most important thing I could do was surround myself with people who care, and can be trusted.

"I closed my comments by asking people to go back to their offices and look for their job descriptions, find them, then tear them up. I closed my comments by saying, 'From this day forward, there are only two jobs in this company: You either serve the customer directly, or you serve someone who does.'

"The audience was stunned into silence for a few moments, then burst into applause. In fact, I got a standing ovation! And from that day forward, 'Serve the Server' has been part of our culture. Everyone can nominate individuals who have gone above and beyond the call of duty to serve customers, or serve someone who does. At our Peak of Performance meetings, we give out national Serve the Server award recognition to four people who exemplify this ideal.

"So to sum up, I think leadership is all about passion, vision and trust. But even more so, I think leadership should be synonymous with the word *serve*. Serving someone in the best manner possible, and always having a mindset built around the concept of service is, to me, what the purpose of leadership is ultimately all about."

71

CHARLES GOLDSTRUCK, PRESIDENT
RCA Music Group
Make decisions decisively.

"Good decision making is virtually always predicted on a thorough review of all the facts surrounding a situation," says Charles Goldstruck, president of the RCA Music Group. "I have found that my decision-making performance is always at its highest when I take the time to thoroughly review every angle of what's affecting the issue being considered.

"However, ultimately, most decisions also are cloaked by subjective factors that require an intuitive feel. These are elements that are normally not immediately obvious but require some level of intuition.

"It is the combination of the aforementioned thorough approach coupled with careful consideration of the subjective elements that are so easily missed or ignored. This style is difficult to implement when decisions have to be made quickly. But whether or not there is enough time to review, this rule still applies because every detail is significant.

"Often it's not possible prior to results coming in to know whether a decision was the right one. However, by always paying attention to feedback coming in after a decision is made—whether it is from my management team, my parent company, my employees, retailers, or customers—the general sentiment coming back will invariably give me a sense as to whether or not my decision will hold up.

"An effective mentor needs to set the bar at the highest level possible and always performs consistently so that there are as few mixed messages as possible for those observing. The values that those who follow need to subscribe to in order to elevate themselves to the level of their mentor—namely integrity, honesty, competence, determination, vision, and trust—should always be upheld.

"Even though no leader is infallible, one is generally judged more by failures than successes, and thus one cannot afford to lower the bar.

"As a leader of people, the ability to make decisions decisively is critical. Procrastination and fear of making the wrong decisions create uncertainty in an organization and ultimately cause bottlenecks in the management chain of any company, large or small.

"One of our divisions, RCA Records, secured the recorded music rights to the American Idol television franchise. Our plan was to release both singles and full albums from the show's winner and runner-up. This year's show began on January 21 and ended on May 21. During that broadcast period, the field of contestants was winnowed down from nearly 8,000 initial participants to the 10 finalists and then of course to the overall winner.

"The need for our company to be agile in this case cannot be overstated: Within two weeks of the show's finale, we would release commercial CD singles to the public for Ruben Studdard and Clay Aiken, the winner and runner-up, respectively. During the same time, we were releasing and promoting 2002 winner Kelly Clarkson's full-length album, as well as that of Justin Guarini, the runner-up. Rounding out the picture was a compilation album containing the favorite song of each of this year's ten finalists. So while it was an exciting picture for all of us, the risks were clear to everyone.

"Time was of the essence. The American Idol music franchise was potentially worth $100 million in sales to the RCA Music Group in 2003. To get there, we needed to take full advantage of the show's huge television audience, especially given that Fox was shattering all of their previous television audience records.

"In January, I made the decision that the release dates for all American Idol products would be set in stone well in advance, and that we would stick to them. The risk here, of course, was that we could be caught short if we could not meet extremely tight recording deadlines. Failure would mean the risk of millions of dollars in marketing commitments then put in place.

"Such decisiveness at the outset, I think, created full understanding in our company not only of my commitment to the franchise, but also made clear my absolute determination to meet our deadlines by any means. And thanks to a superhuman effort on the part of every employee involved, Kelly Clarkson's album debuted at #1 on the *Billboard* charts; Clay Aiken's did the same on the singles chart, with Ruben Studdard's single only a hair's breadth behind. That success has spawned enormous anticipation for Ruben and Clay's full albums, both slated for release in October/November. If I had not been decisive from the outset, our release plan could have easily strayed, with damaging results.

"Learn how to accept constructive feedback, from senior business partners as well as from peers and subordinates. For improving performance and sharpening one's skill set, there are few qualities more effective. Exposure to criticism can be difficult, of course, but if handled gracefully, it is a recipe for a smooth, confident management style and ultimately strong leadership qualities.

"Also, be an effective and careful observer of others. I have always found it extremely helpful to follow the examples set by various mentors who have guided me throughout my career. Paying attention to the strengths and weaknesses of successful executives allows one to incorporate the best practices and habits of those who have accomplished in their careers what each of us strives for."

72

BRUCE BENT II, CEO
Reserve Funds

Find your own way of doing things.

"I never thought of myself as having a secret or using a technique," says Bruce Bent of Reserve Funds, "but what I do most often is try and get the people I work with to see what I'm seeing, to see the vision I have for the company. Some people just get it right away; they think similarly to the way I think, they see the potential of the company the way I do, and they see the nature of the business world in general as I do.

"But most people have a perspective and vision that is a fraction of the whole, either because of their skillset and interests, or by virtue of having a very focused role in the grand scheme, contributing to a segment of the whole, like a welder halfway through an assembly line.

"When I convey my vision, I always try and start from the top down. I start with the big picture in plain English, but I don't necessarily put it all in layman's terms. I use a certain degree of technical language because it makes sense to educate people—it's a good investment of time, and the primary by-product is that nobody feels as if I'm talking down to them.

"Of course I explain what things mean if eyes glaze over. I usually get through the big picture pretty quickly, because if it's not quick, it means it's not simple. And if it's not simple, it means you've probably got a flaw in the plan.

"We've only got 115 employees, all in the same office, so it's easy for me to learn as much as I want about individuals. How people do this with 10,000 employees I have no idea, and I never want to run a company like that anyway.

"When some commonsense employees become inspired by and attached to the vision, they constantly question the route to the goals, which is great for someone like me. I never feel like I have everything nailed down; I always feel like I'm screwing up, missing a piece, or at the very least, not executing in the best way possible.

"This makes me open to the mailroom clerk who says, 'At the last meeting, you said our retail clients were our most profitable clients and we wanted to grow that part of the business, so why don't we advertise in the *New York Post?*' He's right; lots of our clients and prospects read the *New York Post,* so why don't we advertise there?

"Maybe we should, and maybe we shouldn't. The thing is, he brought up a great question, and I'll find the answer to it if I don't know it already. Then whether I give that guy the answer right there in front of everyone else, or I send it to him in an e-mail a month later, everybody wins. The answer helps me refine the goal. It shows him that I care about his ideas, and that he is valued beyond sorting the mail. And it tells everyone else in the room the same thing, creating a little more mutual respect.

"I always feel like I owe it to the people who are working toward the vision to make sure most everyone else is too. If we find people who are not with us, we try and make an adjustment. And if we fail, they go. To protect the company is to make sure the people who do a great job are treated with respect. One important way to do that is make sure their coworkers support them. If they are making the effort but hit obstacles, you must remove the obstacles, to continue their feeling of accomplishment, to continue their experience of forward motion and success. Be it people or things, you have to continually clear the path for productive people to deliver.

"The most powerful thing you can do is be real. People will respect it and respond to it. Sincerity and honesty will illuminate your opportunities and your obstacles. I believe this is a spiritual phenomenon. It will not automatically bring success, but it will reveal the truth of the path before you. Then, if you make good judgments about how to handle what you see, you will most likely succeed. Do this in your own way; be comfortable with your own style. If you sacrifice your own personal approach to things, even your personal style, you sacrifice some of your power and your integrity.

"Recently I sat down before an arbitrator and an army of high-priced attorneys on both sides to resolve a dispute with an organization ten times our size. I was told to be prepared for a battle that would last at least all day, if not a few days. I made the first opening statement after the arbiter said his piece, and we were done in two hours. I asked why things were moving so quickly and why they seemed so pleased. They told me that the honesty of my opening statement eliminated the majority of the confrontation and the time that went along with it.

"I didn't say, 'Hey, you can have what you want, do what you wish with me, I'm weak.' I didn't say, 'If we're not out of here in the next fifteen minutes, I'm going to spend the rest of my life pursuing you and your families.' I said, 'Here's how I see it, here's what's important to me, here's what will work, and here's what will just piss me off.' I gave everyone a clear road map to success, achieved my goals in the process, and we all got back to work before lunch.

"Find your own way of doing things, don't imitate others, and find what works for you. Making things happen and leading others is totally personal. I know people that can walk into a room full of strangers, and just by their presence and the sound of their voice, get people to do what they want. I can't do it that way. I need to get people to click with the vision and when they do, they become almost self-motivated."

73

AUDREY OSWELL, PRESIDENT AND CEO
Resorts Atlantic City

Be visible.

"Be visible. Talk to your customers. But more important, talk to your employees. Eat in the employee cafeteria, if you have one," suggests Audrey Oswell of Resorts. "Employees are the core of any organization. They make your business tick and they know what makes your customers tick. Your employees know your customers' likes and dislikes. They also can easily identify barriers to delivering great customer service. Regardless of the type of business you are in, employees hold the key to customer satisfaction.

"When I first took my current position, business had declined by more than 25 percent from the prior year in a market where revenue growth had been flat for the past two years. The owners and senior management of the company gave me many reasons for why business had fallen off. My first day of work I developed a sense that I had not heard the whole story. Employees seemed unusually distrusting of management and somewhat hostile.

"So, I started talking to the employees and eating in the employee cafeteria. At first the employees were hesitant to talk to me, so I just listened. It didn't take long until I was able to open up a dialogue and obtain the information I needed: Why did our customers defect?

"In the employee cafeteria I seemed more approachable; it was a less threatening environment, their turf. Very quickly they started opening up to me and the stories I heard from them were very different from the ones senior management were telling.

"Then I started talking to customers and it turns out the employees were right in determining why business had fallen off so dramatically. Because I listened to the employees, the turn around of the business was much quicker. The execution was flawless, because the employees were on board.

"Know what you know and know what you don't. Don't be above reaching out for advice and other opinions. Listen to others, but in the end the decision remains yours. Be sure to include your front line employees in the mix of those you seek information from."

74

LLOYD G. "BUZZ" WATERHOUSE, CEO

Reynolds & Reynolds

Simplify until it fits on one page.

In an increasingly complex world, Buzz Waterhouse, CEO of Reynolds & Reynolds, believes the key to effective leadership is to keep things simple.

"I believe great leaders are great simplifiers," says Buzz. "After all, leaders lead people, not organizations or companies. And leading people is about gaining understanding, alignment, and support. One of the best ways to do that is to simplify."

Buzz outlines the three key questions every leader must ask himself:

1. Does everyone understand the direction you're headed and how you expect to get there?
2. Are your people aligned around that direction?
3. How can you gain their support for the actions needed to move in that direction?

"I try hard to simplify things to their essence," Buzz says. "My approach to solving any problem is to synthesize the facts until I can find the essence of what the company is trying to do."

The key to his method: *Simplify the business plan until it fits on one side of a sheet of paper.*

"It doesn't matter whether it's the most complex business or complicated market, an organization's core values, or any other critical focus. Simplify it to one page. That way, everyone in the organization is—

literally—working from the same page. They see the same picture, and use the same language to talk about the essence of what you're doing. And then you hammer it home in everything you do.

"In my career, I've worked with leaders who have been extraordinarily good as simplifiers in the most complex, global businesses you can imagine. That ability makes an enormous difference. I've also worked with leaders who made the simplest business too complex, and it drove most of us nuts. It also made us less effective.

"Both experiences have stayed with me and reinforced the same lesson: A leader's ability to simplify is a powerful way to focus people on the essence of what you're doing."

Reynolds & Reynolds serves automobile retailers with information technology and software. The technology enables these dealerships to manage their businesses more robustly and connect seamlessly with car companies and with consumers.

Recently they developed a new technology platform that captures a comprehensive picture of an automobile retailer's entire business and all the touch points with consumers—from the first visit to the dealer's Web site to the service reminder after 40,000 miles.

Following his philosophy of "keep it simple," Buzz and his executive team managed to articulate the new generation of solutions—and the company's approach to the market—on one side of a single sheet of paper.

"We displayed the essence of what Reynolds offered by grouping solutions around the circumference of a wheel," says Buzz.

"Each section of the wheel, like a slice of pie, represents a department in a dealership and a set of corresponding solutions from Reynolds. Adjacent slices on the wheel are linked, and together form a comprehensive, integrated array of technology solutions that match a customer's total business needs.

"That sounds pretty basic, I know, but the wheel takes two complex businesses—ours and the dealership—and simplifies both. All I have to do is mention the wheel, and everyone in the organization knows the reference point. This simplifies the essence of how we meet the customers' needs and creates value for them in every part of their auto dealership—from sales and leasing, to insurance and financing, to parts and service."

Buzz concludes: "I recall reading a comment made by Einstein. He said, 'Always simplify things to the greatest extent possible, and not one bit more.' That seems like a pretty good formula for business success."

75

BRENT B. JOHNSON, PRESIDENT AND CEO

Ringland-Johnson Construction Co.

*Maximize the strengths and moderate the
weaknesses of your employees.*

"Over the years, I've noticed that good football coaches have a system that is well reasoned, thorough, and adaptable to one's opponent," says Ringland-Johnson's CEO, Brent Johnson.

"Great coaches, however, continually create newer systems to maximize the strengths and moderate the weaknesses of their present roster. 'Three yards and a cloud of dust' would have been a sinful waste of a Joe Namath or John Elway.

"Although sports analogies don't always work, this one stands up to my particular management philosophy. I 'draft' (recruit) people based more upon their overall skills than any one talent. It's the concept of taking the best athlete available and finding a position for him later.

"We do not hire widget-makers; we employ people to work with systems and customers. One-dimensional people don't fit our need situation.

"Once a recruit comes aboard, his or her strengths become clear in short order. It is at that point that we reprogram our original job description to one better suited to our new employee.

"Obviously, these modifications have limits. We won't change our operations solely to accommodate one person. What we will do and have successfully done is to always consider the individual's capacity in assigning his function.

"Organizations that ignore effective people placement do so at their peril. A roster of employees is not necessarily an asset; a coordinated team most certainly is."

76

MICHAEL W. WICKHAM, CEO

Roadway Corporation

Hire and care for good quality people within the organization.

Roadway's Michael Wickham thinks that success in running a company comes from hiring and caring for good quality people within the organization.

"Once you have them hired and cared for," he says, "you must help them stay engaged in pursuing corporate success. To do this, you must have a clear vision of what success means yourself. And you owe it to the people in the organization to clearly communicate that vision and the mission all the way through the company. This gives people a chance to understand and measure their own contribution to the cause.

"When we spun off from our parent company in 1996, it was critical that we regained a focus on our company as a stand-alone. People were very anxious about standing alone as a union carrier in a tough industry.

"We labored hard and long to create and communicate a simple concise mission for our company. We went to Teamster leadership, to rank and file Teamster employees, to our dockworkers and our drivers, to our managers, clerks, supervisors, and mechanics, and laid out the mission before us and the part they played in the overall mission. We also gave everyone measurements they could use to judge their contribution to our effort. We called it *results focused quality*.

"In traveling through the organization—in the offices, the drivers' rooms, and the dock break rooms—it was easy to determine how well the message was being disseminated. It is truly rewarding to walk among the people who do the job and hear your own words come back to you.

"Ours is a very competitive business staffed by proud and competitive people throughout. As a CEO, my responsibility is to do everything I can to make them understand why they are working so hard and to give them measurements that help them know how they are doing.

"A person can learn to be a leader by continually communicating with all levels of people in the business and trying to see things as they do. In my case, I had a few very good bosses and a few very bad ones. I learned from each one and incorporated what I learned into my own style. An effective leader has to have a style that fits his or her personality, and he or she must constantly hone those leadership skills as times and people change.

"Over the years, we have carefully studied our turnover statistics and looked at our successful candidates. From that, we have gained a good understanding of the type of person we should hire, essentially, what qualities they should possess.

"The goals that are set at the local level, and even the individual level, are set with a full understanding of what the corporate goals are. The setting of individual and group goals is done collaboratively. We are constantly communicating and discussing our goals and our results throughout the organization.

"My best boss had enormous integrity and allowed me to share in the 'thrill of victory' when we were successful, but also allowed me to share the 'agony of defeat.' In both cases, it was a shared emotion and one that lead to the planning and deployment of tactics to continue and improve. I always had a plan that he helped me put together to reach the next step.

"There will always be disappointing results; I have learned that. I have also learned that there is great comfort and a feeling of security that comes from having a plan to improve those results.

"The one thing I learned from my worst boss was that an organization is badly weakened by a top down blame game approach to adversity. With no collective plan going forward, various elements of the team operate independently of each other and simply try to look good—or worse, make others look bad.

"From these observations in business and team sports, I developed my style, which is collaborative and supportive, while still remaining focused on results that are realistically attainable."

77

HAROLD M. "MAX" MESSMER, JR., CEO

Robert Half International, Inc. (RHI)

Quickly turn creative ideas into successful business practices.

Robert Half International's CEO points to a *Business Week* article published in 2002 that referred to him as the "contrarian."

"This is probably an apt description," says Harold "Max" Messmer. "I haven't always followed industry convention. I believe you must cultivate a questioning attitude and be willing to take calculated risks in business. I've tried to instill this same entrepreneurial spirit in the people who work with me.

"Several years ago, I wrote an article for a business publication that highlighted the importance of encouraging innovative thinking. The most discouraging thing a manager can do is to relegate the creative suggestions of his or her employees to the *No Zone Layer*. This is a term we've coined to describe the place where valuable ideas are lost because management is afraid to challenge existing ways of thinking.

"The ability to quickly turn creative ideas into successful business practices has always been the cornerstone of a company's success. A progressive culture cannot afford a status-quo approach.

"While corporate values should remain constant, procedures and business processes must continually evolve in order to meet changing market demands. Welcoming fresh ideas by cultivating an environment that not only allows, but also promotes and rewards, prudent risk taking makes sound business sense.

"It is also important to aggressively test new ideas in order to continually improve upon them. This is a strategy we have implemented many times at Robert Half International when we have introduced new service lines or entered new markets. The most far-fetched or seemingly impossible approach can spur others to think creatively and often leads to solutions that would otherwise never have been considered.

"For those who are concerned about jeopardizing order and control in creating a culture that encourages risk taking, consider the alternative: the possibility of dismissing potentially powerful and transforming ideas. Those who have been told their idea holds promise but would be too difficult to implement know firsthand how frustrating and discouraging these words can be.

"At RHI we have a 'what a good idea' program that encourages employees throughout the organization to submit ideas for improving service and productivity. Establishing and nurturing an environment that embraces risk taking is not an easy task, but the rewards are immense. The most satisfied and productive people in any organization are those who feel they are allowed to participate fully and who know that their contributions are valued.

"The decision to acquire Robert Half Incorporated came as a surprise to many. My associates and I had no experience in staffing, but we admired the franchise business that the founder, Robert Half, built. Mr. Half had pioneered the concept of specialized accounting and finance staffing.

"When he launched the company in 1948, it was the first recruiting firm of its kind to focus exclusively on accounting positions. When Accountemps was created in 1974, it was the first business to specialize in placing accountants on a temporary basis. Prior to that, temporary positions were primarily clerical or light industrial in nature.

"Our goal was to take a well-known franchisor and build a company-owned operation by acquiring the independent franchises. At a time, when franchising successful businesses was popular, it was not as common to pursue the reverse strategy.

"Nonetheless, over the next several years we acquired most of the franchised operations in 48 transactions representing nearly 100 offices, and we did so without being involved in litigation. In fact, a number of the franchise owners stayed with the company. Early in 2003, we acquired the final two franchises and RHI is now 100 percent company owned and operated.

"Once we had acquired the majority of the original franchises and had staffing operations that were predominantly company-owned, we made the decision to focus almost exclusively on growth through internal expansion. We resisted the temptation to increase revenues through the acquisition of other staffing firms, which was a popular strategy in our industry during the 1990s. We instead focused on becoming the leader in specialized staffing by expanding from within.

"In the process, RHI has grown from $7 million in operating revenues in 1986 to $1.9 billion in 2002, virtually all of which is the result of organic growth. For the ten years ended December 31, 2002, RHI ranked in the top 1.5 percent of all NYSE firms trading during this period based on total return. The company was also in the top 2.5 percent of the S&P 500 based on total return over this same period, underscoring the company's performance over the long term.

"As we built RHI, we saw an opportunity to take the concept of professional-level temporary staffing and apply it to other professional disciplines such as the legal, technology, and creative and advertising fields. This was also an untested strategy, and many were skeptical. They felt that while companies regularly used temporary workers for less skilled positions, demonstrating the viability of using contract professionals at higher skill levels would be a challenge.

"The concept of employing professional-level temporaries for specialized projects was still foreign to most businesses in 1986 when we acquired Robert Half Incorporated. Companies hired temporary workers to fill in for absent or vacationing clerical or light industrial workers, but had not considered the benefits of bringing in interim assistance at higher skill levels. This concept has taken hold and today professional-level staffing is the fastest-growing segment of our industry.

"We also introduced the concept of strategic staffing, in which companies incorporate the use of temporary employees into their annual budgets to accommodate anticipated and unanticipated workload peaks and special projects. We advise companies to maintain a mix of full-time and temporary professionals for greater flexibility in responding to variable resource needs.

"As we have grown, we have kept our specialized approach—each of our seven professional staffing divisions has a separate focus, separate branding, and separate employee teams. For example, many of our recruiters who place legal professionals are themselves attorneys and legal administrators. This ensures they understand their clients' needs.

"Similarly, we hire accountants to place accountants and creative professionals to place marketing, design, and advertising specialists. This specialized approach has served us well, as it enables us to provide a higher level of service to the companies we work with and the professionals we place.

"In 2002, we took a chance on a new subsidiary. We launched an internal audit and risk consulting business called Protiviti after hiring more than 700 former partners and other professionals formerly with Arthur Andersen. This was at the height of the corporate accounting scandals of 2002.

"We saw a unique opportunity to enter a market in which we had long wanted to participate more fully, with individuals experienced in providing internal audit and risk consulting services to leading firms worldwide. The former Andersen professionals we hired were in separate practices from Andersen's external audit and attestation services and had no involvement in activities related to the widely publicized Enron litigation.

"This business has proven to be a strong complement to our professional staffing services and is quickly becoming a recognized leader in business and technology risk consulting and Sarbanes-Oxley Act compliance. Protiviti, a wholly owned subsidiary of RHI, focuses on the rapidly growing areas of internal audit and business and technology risk consulting.

"The business potential for this subsidiary quickly became apparent last year as corporate accounting scandals underscored the need for auditor independence and increased corporate governance, areas in which our consultants are uniquely qualified to provide expert guidance. With respect to Sarbanes-Oxley compliance, Protiviti is competing successfully with the Big Four accounting firms to provide internal audit services to public companies.

"New regulations mandate that a public company's external auditor cannot also provide internal audit services to that company. This has left an opportunity for Protiviti to provide these services. Section 404 of Sarbanes-Oxley requires publicly traded companies to establish an internal audit function and ensure proper internal controls over financial reporting, and we are working with a rapidly growing number of companies to help them comply with these requirements.

"The name Protiviti represents professionalism, integrity, and objectivity. Protiviti began operations with 25 locations in major U.S. markets, and within nine months had also established a presence in Paris, London, Tokyo, and Singapore to better serve our global client base. We have been very pleased with the rapid growth and market acceptance of Protiviti has gained in its first year of operation.

"There is a significant difference between being a manager and being a leader. Leading is more than simply delegating tasks and ensuring your employees are busy. Leaders inspire excellence in the people who work for them and motivate them to perform their best work.

"If you are already in a management role, assess whether you are a leader or simply a manager. Look for ways to motivate your staff and ask for honest feedback from peers about your supervisory style. Be willing to accept constructive criticism.

"Leaders demonstrate initiative. Volunteer for projects that fall outside your job description to gain new skills. This will take you out of your comfort zone. If you have significant experience in a particular field, industry or specialty area, become a mentor to someone.

"There are many who could benefit from your experience and expertise. By serving as a mentor, you'll enhance leadership abilities such as interpersonal communication and collaboration. You'll also gain satisfaction in knowing you've helped someone advance his or her career.

"Leaders must be task-oriented while also providing a vision for employees and establishing a path for realizing that vision. To become better leaders, managers should continually focus on strategy as well as execution.

"Companies should also invest in building leadership talent from within. In an RHI survey of 150 executives from the nation's largest companies, leadership skills were identified as the most valued asset in managers. Still, many companies face shortages in critical leadership talent.

"Building leadership skills from within is essential to grooming a company's next generation of managers and senior executives. At RHI, we provide employees with continual training opportunities to enhance career advancement.

"Through RHI University, our professional development program that combines classroom and Web-based instruction, our employees participate in activities designed to build leadership, management, technical, and communication skills.

"We have developed one of the most comprehensive and advanced professional development programs in our industry and have made a commitment as a company to continually invest in ongoing educational opportunities for employees at all levels.

"In business, certain people do appear to have innate management capabilities, while others possess what could be called leadership potential. For the second group, this potential can be developed so that they, too, become confident and competent managers.

"There is a Greek proverb that says, 'Without a general, an army is lost.' The same principle applies to businesses: Without strong leadership, they will fail, making it imperative that firms develop individuals who can lead their companies."

78

DANIEL ROSE, CHAIRMAN
Rose Associates, Inc.

Convey a compelling vision of what you believe your group
can accomplish, and contagious enthusiasm can encourage
them to achieve more than thought possible.

"A leader should be able to convey a compelling vision of what he believes his group can accomplish, and contagious enthusiasm can encourage them to achieve more than thought possible," says Daniel Rose of Rose Associates, which develops and manages quality commercial, retail and residential properties throughout the eastern seaboard with projects in New York City, Connecticut, and the greater Boston area. The company manages nearly 30,000 residential units and four million square feet of commercial space, and is one of the largest managers of street-level retail space in Manhattan.

"In presenting to my team the exciting but realistic prospects for the development of the Pentagon City complex in Arlington, Virginia, or in conveying to a skeptical theatrical community what the Manhattan Plaza development could mean for housing for the performing arts in New York, I was able to convert neutrals into allies.

"Pentagon City eventually won the Urban Land Institute's coveted award for the Best Mixed Use Development in the nation because, among other things, of its complexity, which was frightening to some.

"At the very outset, it was necessary to demonstrate to skeptics that each individual component was doable, that the components could be orchestrated comfortably together, and that, at the end of the day, the varied characteristics were mutually supportive and that the resulting synergies would benefit all concerned.

"Anyone can learn to state his message simply, clearly, and—if he believes it himself—with passionate conviction. And that is half the battle.

"I believe that leadership can be learned by studying examples of successful leaders in a variety of professional fields. Whether it is Pericles to the Athenians in his Funeral Oration or Julius Caesar in his Commentaries, Henry V before Agincourt or Winston Churchill during the Battle of Britain, great leaders are able to inspire, encourage, and embolden their fellows to achieve more than they thought they could.

"We know virtually nothing about Genghis Khan or Attila the Hun, but I would bet anything that they sent their armies into battle fired up with enthusiasm. Saddem Hussein's sons tried torture to get Iraq's Olympic athletes to win—and in the very short run that is undoubtedly a great stimulus. But Stalin and Hitler, pragmatists both, found that rewards, praise, and encouragement worked much better in the long run.

"George Washington and Franklin D. Roosevelt dealt remarkably well with the problems they faced, and today's governmental types should study their approaches. Today's business leaders face different types of problems, of course, but the ability to convey a compelling vision remains."

79

THOMAS C. SULLIVAN, CHAIRMAN

RPM International Inc.

Hire the best people you can find. Create an atmosphere
that will keep them. Then let them do their jobs.

"What is my powerful leadership secret or technique?" asks RPM's chairman, Thomas Sullivan. "Actually, it's a business philosophy that my father, Frank C. Sullivan, imparted to me. He always said, 'Hire the best people you can find. Create an atmosphere that will keep them. Then let them do their jobs.'

"When he died in 1971, the company, then known as Republic Powdered Metals, had annual revenue of about $11 million and net income of $600,000. During the next 30 years, we were able to grow the business to $2 billion with net income of more than $100 million by consistently applying this philosophy.

"Shortly after my father's death, we began growing RPM by adding acquisitions to our internal growth. RPM has been a very effective consolidator in the specialty coatings industry, with more than about 100 total acquisitions and 60 since 1991. We applied my father's philosophy about people to the companies we acquired. That is, 'buy the best companies you can find, create an atmosphere that will keep their key people, then let them do their jobs.'

"All seven individuals who lead our operating management team came to RPM via acquisitions. Today, each of them has vastly larger areas of responsibility and attendant compensation than they did when they joined RPM.

"For example, Jeff Korach joined the company in 1984, when we acquired the $12 million Euclid Chemical Company, a family business.

Today, Jeff runs our largest entity, the Tremco Group, with sales of approximately $450 million.

"Mike Tellor joined RPM in 1985, when we acquired the Carboline Company, where he was vice president-international. When we bought Rust-Oleum in 1994, none of the Ferguson family, which owned the business, wanted to remain with it. We sent Mike in to run it. At that time, Rust-Oleum produced a single, limited line of rust-preventative paints sold in small packages. Today, it is the category leader in small package paints, adding decorative, general purpose, and specialty coatings to the original rust-preventative line. Sales have more than tripled under Mike's stewardship.

"In corporate management, we have built an extremely solid younger management group averaging 45 years of age and nine years of service to RPM. Leading this group is my son, Frank C. Sullivan, who became CEO of RPM at our annual meeting in October 2002. This group has proved its mettle by implementing the only restructuring program in our history, which was conducted from August 1999 through our fiscal 2001 third quarter, ended February 28 of that year. The restructuring involved reducing the work force by 10 percent, consolidating manufacturing and distribution and combining certain product lines. While the restructuring was painful, our financial results since its completion validate the effectiveness of this effort. RPM's net income exceeded $100 million for the first time in fiscal year 2002 and grew another 21 percent during fiscal 2003, prior to a charge for potential asbestos-related liabilities.

"I'm not sure leadership can be taught. Having said that, I do believe that people who have a natural knack for leadership can certainly augment their skills in this area tremendously, through several steps. One is to have a voracious appetite for reading and to learn from the successes and failures of others. Certainly, the large number of excellent business books and periodicals provides an abundance of information in this regard.

"Another step is to be prepared to learn from anyone. Leaders who discount the opinion of someone who may not be terribly high up on the corporate totem pole deny themselves an opportunity to learn. Likewise, there are significant opportunities to learn by serving on boards of not-for-profits, as well as private and publicly held companies.

"It's also important to have your finger on the pulse of your marketplace. Trade and professional groups provide an excellent source of this input. Mass media give insight to changing consumer behavior patterns.

"Finally, and perhaps most importantly, a leader needs to be passionate about his or her cause, company, or organization. Throughout history, passion has overcome shortfalls in knowledge and experience. Those with strong passion can inspire others to follow them.

"One book I've recently read is *The Rise of the Creative Class* by Richard Florida. It discusses the ever-increasing need for human capital and helped reinforce my belief in RPM's founding philosophy: Go out and find good people, create the atmosphere to keep them, and let them do their jobs.

"RPM is not a family business. It is a publicly traded company with some 100,000 shareholders and a board of directors dominated by independent directors for the past quarter century. But, with three generations of Sullivans at the helm, the question of nepotism does have merit.

"I have not run into this issue during my tenure for three key reasons. The first is that RPM has a culture of treating all employees equally and fairly. Additionally, family members, like all other employees, are hired based on matching their abilities to a given job's requirements. Family members are then held to the same conditions of employment as any other employee, including advancement, promotion, compensation, and, if necessary, termination.

"Second, like my father did before me, I had all of my six children spend time working for RPM in various capacities while growing up. In doing so, my short-term goal was to instill in them a strong work ethic and respect for the business. My long-term goal was that should any of them desire to work for RPM as adults, they would have developed an intimate knowledge of how the company operates and a strong passion for the business. This knowledge and passion would help them succeed.

"Third, we like to say that 'nepotism at RPM is not a dirty word.' Family involvement in RPM does not only take place at the corporate level, but also with the operating companies. For example, Randy Korach is president of Tremco's Sealants/Weatherproofing Division, and son of Tremco Group President Jeff Korach. Randy has played a large part in Tremco's growth over the past few years.

"Stacy Senior Allan, marketing director of Thibaut Wallcoverings, has helped the small, upscale line of wallcoverings grow revenue in a declining industry. She is the daughter of Bob Senior, head of our Zinsser Group, who oversees Thibaut.

"RPM's effectiveness as a consolidator in the industry and the sheer number of deals we look at over the course of a year have enabled us to know many people in the industry and recognize those with talent. Good people tend to gravitate toward good companies.

"At RPM, we have created a good company. We provide our employees with challenging work, fair base compensation backed by a strong incentive compensation program, a pleasant environment, and opportunity for advancement. Then, we step away and let them perform. This has allowed us to rein in such talent to our operating companies as Peter Balint to Dryvit and Pat Formica to Bondo.

"Prior to joining Dryvit, Peter was vice president of marketing of the Specialty Brands Division of Sherwin-Williams, and Pat was president of Permatex Inc. Some of our corporate officers previously worked for our accounting firm, law firm, or other advisors. This allowed both them and us to size each other up before proceeding to a formal relationship.

"Some of the factors I already mentioned include challenging and rewarding work, fair compensation backed by a strong incentive compensation program, a pleasant environment, an opportunity for advancement, and trust to let employees perform. In addition, RPM has a culture where employees can share their opinions openly and freely.

"We also maintain a collegial atmosphere. This is particularly true at our lean corporate headquarters, but also applies to our operating companies. This atmosphere is created, not through a set of policies, but rather through a corporate culture that is established at the top and is embedded throughout the organization."

80

JAMES W. KEYES, PRESIDENT AND CEO
7-Eleven, Inc.

Teach!

A lot has been written about the importance of knowledge in the business world: knowledge management, the information age, the learning organization, data as a strategic advantage. James Keyes, CEO of 7-Eleven, takes organizational learning very much to heart.

"The most effective means of gaining alignment and execution of my strategic plan is to have my senior management engaged in teaching," says James.

"I discovered long ago that many people are good at repeating the basics of a strategic plan, but their understanding may be shallow. If they don't have a thorough understanding of the strategy, execution will suffer."

James requires his senior managers to educate their teams about the strategy and how to implement it.

"When called upon to teach, senior managers must do several things. First, they must prepare their curriculum. Second, they must clarify any understanding with me before they teach.

"Third, and most important, the senior manager will be challenged by the audience to clarify areas of uncertainty. The ability to respond to such questions will inevitably build the teacher's depth of understanding.

"I have engaged all of my senior management team in a teaching exercise designed to create a cascade effect throughout the company. By teaching their respective department heads, and requiring the same of them to their staff, we have an ability to create a culture that has a greater appreciation for the importance of communication, and a better understanding of our strategic plan."

Under the leadership of James Keyes, and with the assistance of Dr. Noel Tichy, a professor at the University of Michigan, 7-Eleven embarked on a Performance Leadership program.

The goals of the program are to develop:

• A single focus for running the business
• An alignment around 7-Eleven's retail initiative strategy
• A belief in item-by-item management in the stores
• A cohesive management team committed to execution
• Opportunities for leaders at all levels in the firm to articulate their own teachable point of view about what it will take for their organization to win and energize the team

"We worked from the premise that winning companies win by having more leaders at every level of the organization than their competitors. We talked about our business model, how we plan to make money, values (the unifying principles that articulate our core beliefs), energy (the methods and mechanisms for developing ways of energizing our work force around our business ideas and values), and edge (facing reality and making yes/no decisions about strategy, markets, people, and products—the ability to make tough calls fast).

"We started with a group of about 10 executives and became aligned on strategies. These 10 executives then helped teach and share learnings with a group of about 48 high-potential executives who worked in six key business issues over a period of about five months. The process yielded terrific ideas from cross-functional groups, reinforced learnings from the 10 executives, and gained further alignment on strategy and values with an important segment of our management team."

There is an old joke in which a man in New York City asks a newsstand owner how to get to Carnegie Hall. "Practice, my boy," answers the newsvendor. "Practice."

James also puts great stock in practice, especially when it comes to leadership skills: "Practice is the only practical method of improving leadership skills, and is a key to becoming an effective leader.

"Leadership is like learning to swim. One cannot read a book and then know how to swim. One must instead plunge into the water and practice.

"The importance of practice—and teaching—is best exemplified by those who study foreign languages. One can study and learn a foreign language from a book. Upon arrival in that foreign country, however, the student may find himself unable to communicate. There is no replacement for the importance of practice.

"Teaching is a similar experience. The teacher, when delivering a lesson, is actually practicing what he teaches and accordingly gains greater knowledge. For this reason, being a good leader requires practice and being a good teacher. The two go hand in hand."

81

WALTER M. HIGGINS, CHAIRMAN, PRESIDENT, AND CEO

Sierra Pacific Resources

Treat every individual, regardless of who they are, with respect.

"I think the single most important thing I do is literally go out of my way to treat every individual I deal with, regardless of who they are, with respect," says Walter Higgins of Sierra Pacific, energy provider for Nevada and northeastern California.

"I believe the results in the long run will be far better if every person believes that their contributions and opinions are respected. In my heart, I know if I didn't, I would get less desirable results.

"Every now and then, you have to deal with someone you don't like. It takes personal discipline to treat such a person respectfully instead of popping off, but if there is tension, the result will not be as good.

"Keeping your cool in a tense situation is something that can be learned, and to be a leader, you must learn it. You do not have to go with the emotion of the moment. You can feel the emotion, but channel it into constructive action, which is the essence of good leadership.

"Leadership skills must be practiced, just as Tiger Woods is good at golf largely because he practices. There are some people whose natural, interpersonal style allows them to be at ease working with people. Other people may have a natural style less conducive to teamwork, but they too can learn to get along with people.

"The best way to learn leadership is to start working with other leaders and watch what they do. But true leadership starts and ends with respect for other people. People know in an instant if the leader does not respect them. And if they sense this, their desire to perform and achieve will be considerably lower."

82

ADRIEN ARPEL, CEO
Signature Club A, Ltd.

*If you are excited about each new technique, innovation,
or product you create, your passion is communicated to your staff.*

Countless business success books advise us that, to succeed, we must be passionate about what we do. Adrien Arpel, founder of one of the most successful cosmetics companies of all time, agrees.

"My most powerful leadership technique, in a word is passion," says Adrien. "If you are excited about each new technique, innovation, or product you create, your passion is communicated to your staff. I treat each product as the second most important idea since the invention of the wheel—and that's not easy since my 'inventions' are skin treatments, cosmetics, and jewelry.

"But the people who work for me know I truly love the products I develop, and my passion communicates itself to everyone: chemists, purchasing agents, copywriters, package designers, marketing staff, and most of all, the customer. Everyone feels they are part of the team that will make the product a success—and who doesn't want to be on a winning team?"

Yet a leader cannot always defer to the team. "When my core executives don't unanimously agree on an idea I feel strongly about, I trust my gut instinct, and go where my passion for the product takes me. Luckily, I've been right more often than wrong, and since I own my company 100 percent, I am able to make all final decisions.

"My passion (or single-mindedness) led me to make the biggest change of my career: I left the department stores where I had a thriving business, and moved to Home Shopping Network (HSN). I believed that if I could talk to the customer directly—and they could see the passion in my eyes and hear it in my voice—I would be successful. I was one of the first national/international cosmetics companies to move to TV marketing, and today, many years later, my company Signature Club A is still the #1 skin care and cosmetics vendor on HSN."

Wouldn't it have been better to test direct response TV—a field in which she was a novice—on a limited basis before moving away from the familiar, proven channel of department stores?

"Although it wasn't direct response TV, I was a beauty expert on television dating back to Mike Douglas, and have appeared on many national television shows, including the *Today Show, Oprah,* and *Sally Jessy Raphael,*" says Adrien. "I also made regular 'beauty expert' appearances on the most popular daytime talk show, *Live with Regis & Kathie Lee.* I realized that whenever I appeared on TV, the products I featured sold out across the country in chains like Saks and Bloomingdale's. So I had actually tested the waters for years, and in the process I also learned how to create fast, dramatic makeovers in front of a TV audience, something that proved enormously helpful after I made the move to Home Shopping Network.

"I also did extensive book tours on local TV stations across the country while promoting my first beauty book, a #1 *New York Times* bestseller, and again saw the power of TV to move product: in the towns where I appeared, there was always an uptick in sales.

"When I first began on HSN, I still had department store operations. But it became obvious that I could not split my energy and commitments in two directions. The benefits of having HSN as a partner became obvious: I didn't have to pay for a field sales force, expensive store real estate with marble floors and crystal chandeliers, or costly advertising, and I could put the money saved into innovative products, custom packaging, and giving the customer fine department store quality merchandise at direct-sales prices."

How did Adrien get her senior management to buy into switching channels?

"The power of TV to move products became very obvious—not only to myself, but to my staff as well. I wasn't a paid beauty expert during those TV talk show appearances, but the payment came from the amount of merchandise an appearance would move.

"Still, I didn't want to take the opinions of senior management for granted. I made a presentation to my key employees wherein I laid out the facts and figures, discussed what we stood to gain as well as what we stood to lose, and discussed my vision for the growth and future of the company. Plus, everyone knew I felt passionate about making the change."

How can a person learn to become a better leader? "Develop a sense of humor and a sense of trust, and you will create a sense of family," advises Adrien.

"First, share a laugh with your staff. I put in long hours with my key employees (all of whom have been with me for over twenty years—probably an industry record), and the work is intense as well as creative. If you can't share a laugh with those who help make your company successful, the long hours will become a grind, and you won't get the best from your employees—or yourself.

"Second, you must trust the people who work closely with you. That means sometimes you must look the other way. If a diligent worker has a specific problem that is taking her away from work, talk with her about the situation. If you believe in your employee, let her do it her way, and she will get the work done. If you don't trust, then you start to accuse, and that is not the style of a leader. I try to forgive others the way I forgive myself.

"I like to believe my employees know loyalty is a two-way street. They know I am loyal to them, and grateful for their contribution to my success, and I try to show it in thoughtful ways: flowers and gifts for special occasions and to say thank you for a job well-done, presents when grandchildren are born, a birthday cake for each employee (even if they have only been with me a week).

"Our office kitchen is stocked with everything from oatmeal, pretzels, and popcorn, to all kinds of sodas, teas, and coffees. I think a pleasant work environment is important. And, when employees do work with me during lunch or dinner hours, I treat for special meals.

"I also believe that where you work is an important component of how you work. We have very beautiful offices in an elegant Madison Avenue location and building, because I believe it is easier to get and keep a high-caliber employee when you create a beautiful environment for them. After all, this is where employees spend most of their time. And, I provide the proper support staff so people have help getting done what needs to be done.

"I also have executives who are self-motivating, and I believe that is a function of their maturity. There are no 20-year-olds in key management positions—my customers largely skew over 40, and so do my executives.

"Finally, I do believe money is very important, because no matter how much people love you, if they are not paid what they are worth, they will not stay. I believe I pay market prices plus for my employees. After many years, I have a comfort level with my top executives, I value them, and if you value people you want to pay them well."

83

STEPHANIE SONNABEND, PRESIDENT

Sonesta International Hotels

Lead people the way they want to be led.

"I lead people the way that they want to be led," says Stephanie Sonnabend of Sonesta. "I lay out the vision and then work with my people on developing strategies for implementing the vision. Some people can easily translate vision into strategy; others need to be lead down the path to make the connection. My vision is always closely connected to Sonesta's core values, which are:

- Practice high standards of integrity and ethics.
- Value employees as individuals.
- Exceed customers' expectations.
- Service with passion.

"For Sonesta Resorts, we wished to turn a hotel stay into a memorable experience. Our Vice President of Food and Beverage, along with our training team, Training by Design, customized programs to make dining more of an experience. This involved everything from how the food is presented on the plate to how it is served. At two of our beach resorts, we developed private dining on the beach, which has resulted in a number of proposals and weddings.

"My vision for Sonesta's Web page is to turn the medium into two-way communication to develop more of a rapport with our customers. A few years ago, we created a discussion forum to allow guests to communicate directly with us and with each other. We have now created virtual concierge, allowing guests to book online similar services they would book at the hotel, including restaurant reservations, spa treatments, and tickets to local events.

"A person needs to develop and communicate a clear vision and then enroll others in that vision. Others will gladly follow a clearly defined path, especially when they understand how what they do fits into the bigger picture. One must treat every individual differently because some people understand the big picture better than others do. If a person is not a visionary, they can still be a strong leader by being a great communicator and executor of someone else's vision.

"As I get to know my upper management team, I listen to them and determine how directive I need to be. At first, most people want relatively close supervision and support that they are on the right track. After awhile, some people feel comfortable about working autonomously and keeping me informed about what I need to know. Others continue to look for direction and more constant feedback.

"I adjust my management style to the individual. Some people want a regularly scheduled time with me, and others just like to pop in when they want to. Some people want to know how they fit into the vision, and others only care about their specific task.

"Imagine that it is the future (five to ten years from now) and your company turned out exactly how you wanted it to. What would that look like? The vision is the destination. It is not the big picture, because it can be as broad or as detailed as you wish. It defines the direction and paths the company will take. It allows people to understand where the company is going and helps define how it will get there. Any strong company vision includes the big picture, but sometimes it is the small things that shape the direction as well.

"Frequent communication is the key. It starts at the top and works down. If top management feels like they participate in the creation and execution of the vision, they become enrolled and discuss with others. When I visit Sonesta Hotels, I talk about the company in general and the direction we are heading. Our hotels also create their own visions, which are consistent with the corporate one and this gets communicated throughout the hotel.

"In some instances, various departments may also choose to create their own visions, such as a catering department deciding that they wish to provide the most memorable weddings in the area. They talk to the banqueting staff and kitchen crew about what would make that wedding special, and let everyone know what is especially important to the bride and groom and their families and guests. Even though our hotels host hundreds of weddings every year, only one wedding is important to each bride and groom.

"Sonesta's vision is to operate unique hotels in spectacular locations that reflect the culture and environment in which they are located. We would like to grow at a pace of adding one or two hotels per year and increase our brand presence in the United States.

"As a family-run business, we treat our employees as individuals and our guests as friends. We pride ourselves in the longevity of our staff, exceeding guest expectations, our integrity and ethical practices, and providing service with passion. We strive to operate profitably to provide a good return to our shareholders and hotel owners and sustain our growth. We wish to add value to people's lives by creating memorable experiences, and support the communities where we operate."

84

JIM PARKER, CEO AND VICE CHAIRMAN

Southwest Airlines

Be a servant leader.

"Be a servant leader," advises Jim Parker of Southwest Airlines. "I believe that as a leader, one must have a true desire to serve in order to be effective. I see my role as a servant leader as one that encourages employees to always stretch their abilities to the next level so that they will grow in their positions.

"Leaders at Southwest find themselves removing barriers to an individual's success instead of finding reasons to say no. We consistently encourage employees to express their ideas on working smarter and more productively, and then they implement those ideas that work. All of this equates to employees who find positions that allow them to do a job that they are passionate about, and, therefore, they work harder at what they do—which equates in the long run to extreme loyalty and high productivity, as well as an unmatched sense of ownership.

"I believe it would be difficult at Southwest Airlines to select an example of when these practices weren't put into place. Because our people make the suggestions, build the programs, develop the marketing strategies, etc. There isn't much that happens here that doesn't demonstrate these beliefs in action.

"For me, it is always listening more than I speak and, more importantly, hearing what is said and acting on it. At Southwest, much of our strategy is developed at a grassroots level, and our employees know that their opinions and ideas count.

"Also, a good leader is not above doing the job of his or her employees. By stepping into the employee's role, you build a relationship with that particular employee or group of employees, but you also gain an appreciation for that particular job. If you spend time regularly working and talking with people, they will appreciate the fact that you respect them and care for them. They will also not be afraid of you and, if you have the attitude of a servant leader, they will begin to express their opinions, ideas, and dreams to you. This input can be priceless.

"At Southwest, every leader's role is one of creating and nurturing an environment that allows employees to find fulfillment and satisfaction in their careers. This means making sure the right tools are available to do the job, providing access at every level to resources to help them, stimulating them to learn continually, and providing continual growth opportunities for them to move ahead professionally and personally.

"Leaders at Southwest are also team players who actively participate on the team, including performing their share of the work or not just paying lip service to the concept. We all strive to set the example for hard work, and we are challenged to inspire our work groups to always be on the lookout for creative solutions to problems and issues.

"Perhaps more important than any of the above, the leaders of Southwest tend to be people who treat others the way we want to be treated, making requests rather than making demands, and giving suggestions as opposed to giving orders. Using the words *please* and *thank you* and asking someone about their weekend or their family are simple courtesies that mean a great deal, particularly if they are heartfelt. Using common courtesies costs the company nothing but pays off a million times over when it comes to loyalty and enthusiasm for the job. People visiting Southwest are amazed that it is difficult to distinguish a pecking order based on behaviors and attitudes of the employees here.

"During the first Gulf War when the airlines were losing huge amounts of money due to the high cost of fuel, many employees of Southwest insisted on donating money out of their paychecks to help cover our fuel costs.

"After the 9/11 terrorist attacks, when almost every other airline announced layoffs, our employees bombarded leadership with offers to donate money, time, lawn-mowing services, profit-sharing checks, back to the company to ensure our financial health. When all those offers were politely refused, an employee group got together to develop a program that allowed individuals to donate back to the company from 1 to 32 hours of pay over a designated time frame. Pride in this company inspired them to do that out of respect for a company whose leadership had given assurances that costs would be slashed in every way possible in order to preserve jobs.

"Many of the innovations that Southwest has introduced to the industry started off with the inspiration of an employee who, because of the leadership he or she had seen at Southwest, had the confidence to express the idea, and leadership served the company by making the idea happen.

"Southwest has a reputation for hiring employees who are grown into leaders, promoting from within when possible. Therefore, many of our leaders have come up through the ranks of their work groups and can, in fact, perform the jobs required of those reporting to them.

"However, we sometimes tap a strong leader with a great track record to head a group that is outside that particular leader's area of expertise. The thought is that the group will become stronger and more effective when nurtured by the type of environment created by that particular leader. Because this type of leader is often an inspirational one, they quickly gain credibility and respect, regardless of their background. In fact, this type of leader usually has such a great reputation that they are welcomed when they move into new areas."

85

RON SARGENT, CEO

Staples

Get your hands dirty.

Ron Sargent, CEO of office supply giant Staples, advises leaders to, "Get your hands dirty. Before you can be a great leader, you need to understand the inner-workings of the business and where and how the greatest impact can be made. In retail, it is about people—talented associates and satisfied customers.

"My first day as CEO I put on the red shirt and black pants (Staples retail stores uniform), went to a Staples store and spent the day helping customers and working alongside associates. Spending time on the front lines is invaluable to help a company achieve excellence.

"I interact with customers directly on a regular basis, and I encourage all associates at all levels to do so. I answer my own phone and e-mail customers directly. In my first year as Staples CEO, I have worked to rally all 55,000 of our associates around centering everything we do on satisfying customers. Everything in our strategy is built around customers.

"Our Back to Brighton customer service program is the pivotal element in a companywide cultural evolution. Everything we do at Staples is customer-centric. We have pumped-up training, added hours to further increase service levels, and even added team incentives that make it possible for hourly associates to increase their pay by as much as $2 an hour if the store as a whole beats its goals. Sales have increased and customer service metrics are at an all-time high.

"You can't go wrong if the two things you pick to focus on are staying close to your customers and associates. The others are based on the needs of the business.

"Whatever you pick, make sure you clearly communicate the goals and objectives across the company, and that you have the ability to execute on the plan. Keep it simple—to a handful of priorities—otherwise you can get distracted and add complexity. I call it complexity creep.

"There is no silver bullet for being a better leader. It is about never underestimating the power of appreciation, picking a few things and doing them really well, and having a deep understanding of your customers and your business."

86

BARRY STERNLICHT, CHAIRMAN AND CEO
Starwood Hotels & Resorts Worldwide

Innovate or die!

For Barry Sternlicht of Starwood, staying in business means "you either constantly innovate or you die. A focus on innovation at all levels of an organization, from the front lines to the executive suite, is what elevates companies to greatness, engaging the organization to respond to a constantly changing world and tough competitive landscape.

"I work hard to create a culture that rewards associates to think about unique ways we can distinguish our hotel brands from our competitors. I appreciate even the wackiest of suggestions, because it shows that people are being creative and are fearless enough to share their ideas. And you know what, sometimes wacky works!

"Great innovations are often instinctual and simple. Sometimes an idea is so different or out-of-the-box that it is hard to even test. You just have to go for it.

"I am relentless when it comes to removing complacency. If your mantra is constant change, raising the bar, then you can never be satisfied.

"One of my best traits and my worst traits is that even the day we launch a successful new product or open a hotel that really breaks the mold, no matter how many accolades it receives, I'm already harping on about our next big thing or what we would do to push the envelope further next time.

"The creation of the new brand of W Hotels is an example of instinctual innovation. Before I entered in the hotel business, I was a typical business traveler. During that Road Warrior phase, I never found a hotel that truly catered to me or the sensibilities of a young, hardworking executive who thought traveling should actually be enjoyable.

"If I stayed at the best hotel in town, I'd marvel at the grandeur, but it was kind of formal and I was scared to touch anything. Or I'd try a hip boutique, which looked great, but the service was abysmal—your breakfast would arrive at dinner or a fax would disappear. And the big hotel brands seemed so bland and undifferentiated.

"When I founded Starwood, I thought there was a huge opportunity to develop a new hotel brand that was not only very stylish and fun, but also offered great service and business amenities. When the first W opened, most colleagues in the industry thought W would be a one-hit wonder, or a passing trend. But now, four years later, we've opened our 17th W hotel, and 18, 19, and 20 should open this year.

"The W brand is considered by many to be the most successful new brand in hotel history. According to an article in *Business Week* (November 20, 2000), 'W Hotels, a hip boutique brand launched by Sternlicht two years ago, is widely regarded as one of the industry's most successful.'

"My goal with W was to cure all my pet peeves about hotels—bad beds, K-Mart art, tiny TVs hidden in huge armoires placed at angles you had to be a contortionist to watch, bad showers, thimble sized generic shampoo, tiny desks, cafeteria restaurants, and dreary bars all in bland, uninspiring surroundings.

"I wanted to create a hotel brand that not only looked cool, but also functioned. I had had one too many bad experiences at boutique hotels that looked awesome, but had terrible service—room service that never arrived, missing faxes, or staff with attitudes. So with W, I set out to merge style and substance.

"The introduction of the Heavenly Bed was another innovation of which I'm proud. I could never understand why hotels, in the business of selling sleep, offered such awful beds—foam mattresses, cheap pillows, polyester bedspreads, and so on.

"I loved my bed at home, so I thought, why can't we put a bed like this in our hotel rooms? I wanted a white duvet, and the operations guys said, 'No way, white is a big no-no in a guest room.'

"I told them to figure it out, and they did: the Westin Heavenly Bed—an all-white, downy bed with awesome pillows and luxurious linens—has been an enormous success. It has not only lured guests to Westin from its competitors, but folks are willing to pay extra just for a great night's sleep.

"Learn to be a better leader by keeping your intellectual humility and allow yourself to constantly learn. Never assume you have all the answers or rest on your laurels. Pay attention to the advice of others.

"Read everything you can get your hands on. I read every magazine you can imagine, from *Business Week* to *Vanity Fair* to *Wired,* and I am constantly ripping out stories of people I find inspiring, ideas I think are neat, or products that catch my eye.

"I read constantly—when I'm on the phone, eating lunch, commuting to work, and especially when I'm flying. I never get on a plane without a huge duffle bag full of the magazines and press clippings I pile on my office floor between long trips, plus a novel or a new design book. I pretty much spend my entire time in the air reading, and with the amount I travel, that's a lot of hours.

"When I travel to hotels, I always make time to chat with the associates and guests at the door or the front desk associates. They are just a wealth of information and a great source of ideas. Be a part of the world and your organization—not an observer.

"And constantly raise your goals, because you may achieve them. Remember that hope is not a business strategy and to a leader, doing pretty good is never good enough. Excellence demands excellence from the top."

87

MARCY SYMS, CEO
Syms

Be as close to impartial as you can in making decisions.

Marcy Syms tries not to make up her mind before she has as many facts as can be collected. "And I try to be as close to impartial as any of us can ever be in making decisions that are best for the company, and ultimately best for our customers," she says.

"For instance, we originally sold men's clothing only. Evolving into women's and children's clothing went against our gift, but it was best for our customers.

"We realized that what our customers want most from us is brand-name clothing at discount prices, no matter what the category. Today we've expanded to sell sheets, pillows, domestics—whatever great brand-name merchandise we can get at discount prices. Our store prices for everything we sell are never more than 10 percent above the wholesale price.

"Our success in children's clothing proved that our brand could extend to almost any merchandise. We've sold leather goods, gift items, watches, eyeglasses, beach games, even baby strollers one year when we got a great deal on them.

"Our advertising says that 'an educated consumer is our best customer.' Our educated consumers are sensitive to the yardstick of quality brand merchandise at discount prices, and that's what they expect to get at Syms.

"If you look on the Internet, there are probably more Web sites on leadership than on any other aspect of business management. Characteristics of a good leader include consistency, fortitude, perseverance, energy, enthusiasm, and the ability to stay on message.

"As a woman, I am particularly sensitive to stereotyping; I know that decisions appearing to be based on extreme emotion may be perceived as not being well thought out. So when I see a situation heating up and getting too emotional, I try to remove myself from it mentally."

88

HIGINIO SANCHEZ, CEO
Telvista

Start the day with a smile.

"One of the things I have been doing for the past twenty years is to really listen to people," says Telvista's Higinio Sanchez. "Treat everyone you talk with—the security guard, the vice president of a company, your daughter—as important, because they *are* important.

"I run a technology company that connects people one-to-one over the telephone and the Web, and for me, the most important aspect of our business is not hardware or software, it is the *humanware*—the people.

"Leaders are not born. What makes you a leader is *other people*. People make a leader, and we cannot become leaders by ourselves.

"You cannot learn to be a leader. You need to live as a leader to become one. Show yourself to others as you see yourself in the mirror every day—with integrity, humanity, and humbleness. Once you start doing that, you become the kind of person others want to emulate and follow, and then the leader arrives.

"Of course, there are many skills and abilities you can learn from others. You can be 80 years old and still learning. My goal is to learn something new every day for as long as I live.

"As a leader, you must roll up your sleeves and get involved. I say hi to people every morning. The more you talk with people, the more they feel they know you, and the better you get to know them.

"Support your team in every situation. Sometimes you want to be the leader of a company that never has problems. But you need to support your team when things are good and when they are not good, to be there for them whatever the situation. As the leader, you should take all the responsibility and give others all the credit.

"Start the day with a smile. Recently I got into a hotel elevator occupied by three men, who were obviously together but not talking. 'Good morning,' I said. They just stared at me and said nothing back. That's not the right way to act, I thought.

"I almost let it go, because I was afraid of what their reaction would be if I pressed the issue. But I did. 'Hey guys, don't you say *good morning* back when someone says it to you? I know you must have a lot of things on your mind, but change your attitude.' They smiled and laughed. 'Today is a present,' I told them. 'It's a gift from God.'

"Don't rule from the castle; rule from the front lines. Don't stay in your office, which is a very long way from the front line. You need to be on the front line every day. Whatever your company is doing, do it yourself, with your team. Lead by example.

"I always share my weaknesses with my people. They know the things I do not do well. By showing them my weaknesses, I get them to help me become better, and I help them be better, too.

"For nine years I have been giving a motivational speech to all new employees. In this speech, I show a picture of a sperm cell. I tell them, 'When you started life, there were 300 million sperm cells all trying for the same egg, but only one made it. That's you. So we all come to life already being leaders. You were already a leader the moment you were born.'"

89

MELVIN J. GORDON, CEO

Tootsie Roll Industries, Inc.

Know where you want the company to go
and spell out a route to get there.

"Moses is a prime example of how not to lead. In the exodus from Egypt, he did not know where he was going or have a route and timetable for getting there. The result was that it took 40 years to lead the Israelites to the Promised Land. Besides that, he didn't delegate. He carried the heavy Ten Commandments down from Mt. Sinai and almost broke his back, when he had younger followers who could have easily carried the load," says Melvin Gordon, CEO of Tootsie Roll Industries, Inc.

"About a decade ago, I gathered our vice presidents into my office and told them, 'We have no ambition to be the largest company in sales volume in the candy industry, but we are going to direct our efforts to become the most profitable per dollar of sales.' Branded candy had been our company's niche since it was founded in 1896 by an Austrian immigrant who brought the chewy chocolaty recipe for wrapped penny candy to his candy shop in lower Manhattan. He named the candy for his young daughter whose name was Clara, but whose nickname was Tootsie. Thank God he didn't name it Clara Roll!

"A CEO can have all the good intentions in the world of leading his company to the industry's highest profit margins, but it won't happen unless he uses powerful leadership techniques to establish initial high gross margins, and then protects these margins from erosion.

"Here are some of the ways we build in high gross margins on new or existing products: We indoctrinate our Brand Marketing Managers to accept or develop no new products unless the prime gross margin is at or over a predetermined percentage of sales.

"Prime gross margin percentage is computed by subtracting the total costs of all raw materials, wrapping materials, direct labor, and its fringes from net sales to get prime gross margin in dollars, which is divided by net sales to arrive at the prime gross margin as a percentage of net sales.

"The marketing manager works with our cost accountants and production executives making choices to keep costs down, and with sales executives to set prices at which products will sell in volume with the proper prime gross margin (PGM) percentage. Any decrease in PGM won't be tolerated unless it is approved by the Vice President of Sales and Marketing as strategically needed against competition or other overriding reasons. All company officers must sign off on the PGM adequacy of every new SKU adopted for marketing.

"What about maintaining the targeted prime gross margin percentage when raw materials, wrap materials, or direct labor costs rise? When this happens, and it has been happening more frequently lately, we gather our marketing managers, production managers, sales executives, and cost accountants into meetings designed to lower costs of the SKU.

"Sometimes it means reducing the candy weight in a bar or in a bag. Alternatively, it may mean reducing packaging costs by pressure on suppliers or using a less expensive packaging structure. All alternatives are examined to see if we can restore the prime gross margin by cutting costs or occasionally by even raising prices.

"Has this strategy been a success? For the last decade, we had the highest profit after tax of any candy maker. We have more than doubled the after-tax profit of Hershey and our other large competitors, and more than tripled the average profit in the candy industry.

"You've heard the expression, 'He is a born leader.' Leadership skills show themselves at an early age. Just go to any playground and you'll observe early leaders. Some leadership qualities are passed on through heredity; others are developed through environment and the process of living among others. How much comes from each source has never been proven.

"We do know, however, that we have a much better chance to train a person who has previously developed leadership skills than training someone without these skills. We use testing, such as the Predictive Index and the Wunderklic Wonderlic Test, to indicate whether the candidate has such leadership traits as self-starting, problem solving, people motivating skills including empathy, ability to convince others, drive to get things done on time, attention to detail, the ability to delegate, and whether decisions are made by fact or by emotion. These traits are checked during several personal interviews by our executives and by a detailed check of references.

"In short, our experience for over 40 years proves that you can't build much leadership ability into a person who comes to you without the above leadership characteristics. With these characteristics present, leadership training on the job is extremely productive."

90

BART C. SHULDMAN, CHAIRMAN, PRESIDENT, AND CEO

TransAct Technologies Inc.

Call an "audible."

Bart Shuldman's most powerful leadership technique is to call an "audible" at any time and any place when changes occur.

What is an audible? "When a quarterback walks up to the line and sees a different defensive scheme, he calls an audible at the line to adjust his play," Bart explains.

"As the year develops, many things change—competition might come out with a new product or a terrorist bomb might go off that effects your market. A good business leader will look at the change and, if necessary, call an audible and make a necessary change to the plan that is in response to the change in market.

"It is a powerful tool, because in today's business environment, things change rapidly. If a business leader understands that, and makes the necessary changes to accommodate the changes in the market and environment, then success has a better chance of happening.

"A business leader is effective when they understand their limits and that even though plans are well documented and thorough, markets and economies change. And if they make an audible move—if the change is effecting being able to deliver the plan—then they are assured that the business will survive.

"For example, we launched a new technology for our largest market and changed the advertising message and the sales tactics when we learned more about how the market accepted the product. Our change was based on the response by our competition and how our customers reacted to the product. It was new technology for the market, and when we reviewed the competitive response and our customer's response, we were able to change the message to gain awareness and fend off our competitor's tactics against us.

"Understand that you are not flawless and neither is your business plan. Make adjustments when you see the need, and make sure you are involved to the point you can see when adjustments are needed. Nothing is set in concrete.

"Your business plan should go through a constant review throughout the year. It should be measured against the criteria it was first set out to address, and more importantly, it should be measured against the current market and economic climate. While business plans are well thought out, the economic and market climate can change. If the change is big enough to affect the results, then the plan needs to be changed."

91

STEVE BELKIN, CHAIRMAN AND CEO

Trans National Group

Value, empower, and appreciate your staff.

"Value, empower, and appreciate your staff," advises Trans National's Steve Belkin. "I send a birthday card and write a note thanking them for their caring and effort. For the company's 10th, 15th, 20th, and 25th anniversary, we took the entire staff to Bermuda for the day to thank everyone for all their hard work.

Steve's advice for becoming a better leader is the same as his most powerful leadership secret: "Value, empower, and appreciate your staff. Treat them with respect. I encourage them to take risks. To try and fail is better than not trying, as long as they learn and grow from their mistakes. Only if they grow will the company grow.

"I feel and I tell them they are the most important asset of the company. I treat them with respect each day. We also hold companywide, monthly Spirit Committee events. And, we give Tiffany gifts as a thank you to recognize their 1, 3, 5, 10, 15, 20, and 25 years of service.

"The real key is how we treat our employees, because only if they feel valued and appreciated can they know how to value and appreciate the customers."

92

ELIZABETH ELTING, CEO
TransPerfect Translations

Have a service orientation.

Liz Elting's most powerful leadership secret is to, "have a real service orientation with employees and clients. Get feedback from the people you want to influence and use it where appropriate.

"For example, when speaking to clients in biotech and pharmaceuticals, they said they were interested in working with an ISO 9001:2000-certified company. As a result, we are becoming certified, and I anticipate this will increase revenues substantially.

"Let your clients and employees know you care about them. Ask them how to help make the company better. Make employees happy to come for work and stay for years. Make clients happier by solving their problems.

"We ask clients for feedback on every project. I also send each of our more than 1,000 clients a survey every year, and we have changed our business based on things they have told us.

"I also meet with employees on a regular basis. I get their feedback on their jobs, their goals, and how they want to get there.

"Have a vision and goals for the organization. Evangelize them. Communicate your vision and goals to your direct reports, so they in turn can communicate the vision and goal down the line.

"Remind people about what you are shooting for. Demand results. Make sure in advance that people know how they will be measured and evaluated. Measure people's performance daily, weekly, and monthly—and manage and lead them based on those numbers."

93

DONALD L. EVANS, SECRETARY OF COMMERCE
U.S. Department of Commerce

Put your trust in other people and they will trust you.

"Put trust in other people, and by trusting others, I have found that they will trust you," says U.S. Secretary of Commerce, Don Evans. "Nothing is more important to being an effective leader than having an unshakable trusting relationship with those whom you work with and those you lead.

"Another powerful principle that guides me is to let people know I care about them, because I do. My actions are grounded in the belief that we are all here to serve a call greater than self—to make other people's lives better.

"It has been my experience that good leaders are optimistic, positive, have an inspiring spirit, look over the horizon, and believe in long-term and high-impact goals.

"Be a good listener. Let people know that you are concerned about their needs, anxieties, and dreams. By doing so you connect with those you lead in a way that shows you value who they are, what they do, and what is important in their lives and the lives of their loved ones.

"Leadership is about uniting people, bringing people together and showing people your heart. I also think it is very important for leaders to understand the scope and magnitude of their personal responsibility—to clearly understand that each action they take, every decision they make, and the way they conduct their lives is being closely watched by those whom they lead and impacts their lives.

"A leader's actions set the tone, determine the course, and leave behind a record of results for history to ponder. It is important to always be mindful that at the end of the road all you have is your integrity or lack thereof.

"Finally, it is important for leaders to have a set of core beliefs to rely and depend on when faced with difficult decisions. Leaders cannot, and should not, separate themselves from their core beliefs. Mine are my faith, family, friends, and my belief in serving others. Those priorities not only shape me, but are the very basis for the decisions that I make."

94

HENRIETTA HOLSMAN
FORE, DIRECTOR
United States Mint

One idea that changes the world.

U.S. Mint Director, Henrietta Holsman Fore, organized her responses to our interview questions as so:

Ideas that change the world. When you assume a position of leadership, look for one or two big, bold ideas that will change the world and make it better for everyone.

A visionary and practical leader is the key component in leading big, bold innovative change in a company, department, or team. In government, presidential appointees have an average tenure of eighteen months. Therefore, any big, bold ideas that you lead should be important and sustainable enough to transcend your tenure and be continuously improved for a decade after you leave.

Let everyone win. Look for ideas in which change is positive, creative, and sustainable.

Examples of creative, sustainable ideas. At the U.S. Mint, we are in the first phase of a project with the Federal Reserve Bank to provide coins in any denomination, in any quantity, anywhere in the country, overnight. Our goal is to develop a fully integrated supply chain in which billions of coins will be manufactured, tracked, and shipped to order. Everyone from our suppliers to banks and retailers will have better production inventory levels, loads, and ordering and distribution systems. The full implementation of this supply chain will save millions of dollars and months of time, and change how coins move through the nation. Who will benefit? The American people.

Another example of a sustainable idea is the U.S.-Asia Environmental Partnership (US-AEP), a program we created and implemented at the U.S. Agency for International Development (USAID) in 1992. The program has grown stronger and more effective in its second decade.

US-AEP brings together a partnership—government, business, and nonprofit organizations—to solve quality of life problems in Asia. There was a vital need, particularly in the urban areas, to provide clean water to drink and clean air to breathe. We knew that together we could draw on U.S. and Asian partners' strengths to solve these issues. It has been a groundbreaking way to marry technology, policies, and capital to provide solutions to the water, air, and lands of Asia. Since its inception, US-AEP partnerships have resulted in more than $1 billion in U.S. technology and services to Asia.

Becoming a better leader. There are four things that you can do to become a better leader.

1. *Devour books.* You have to read, read, read and learn about leadership and management.
2. *Seek experience.* Leaders become better through experience. Look for positions of leadership at school, at work, and at nonprofit organizations. Your leadership is needed in hundreds of ways, and the experience will enrich your leadership skills.
3. *Surround yourself with a team of leaders.* Build and coach a team. Be a leader of leaders. Help, support, and guide the people around you to become better, so that each member of the team becomes better. For those who question whether surrounding yourself with leaders threatens your own leadership, the answer emphatically is *no*. In fact, the team is strengthened and so is your leadership.

   Keep your eyes open for different types of leaders. Not everyone must be a leader of people. There are leaders of values, of thought and opinion. Look for leaders with different skills to be part of your team.

   Leaders carry the responsibility to ensure succession and the future strength of their organizations. The best leaders recognize their high-potential, high-performing talent and assist them in their career paths. There should be a shared commitment to training, learning, and experience.

4. *Get results.* Leaders must have a vision and be tenacious in pursuing it. Learn how to implement, to execute, and to get the results that change the world.

95

STEVE WADSWORTH, PRESIDENT

Walt Disney Internet Group

*I believe there is inherent leadership in the strength
of a well-organized, focused team.*

"I don't think about leadership as a set of techniques or planned
behaviors or an image. I don't have a particular secret or set of leadership rules that I consciously follow," insists Steve Wadsworth, President
of Walt Disney Internet Group.

"I believe there is inherent leadership in the strength of a well-organized, focused team. If I had to describe my leadership approach, I
would say it is about creating, empowering, and guiding teams that
together will guide our organization to the right solutions.

"I rely on the wisdom of a team to set a clear vision, I rely on the
intellectual capital of a team to develop creative ideas, and I rely on the
resources of a team to execute. My role as a leader is to pull the team
together, lead the team through these critical decisions, and help the
team achieve its best.

"How I do that depends on the situation or challenge the team
faces, but communication is always an essential element. If the business
needs direction, I help the team come together, work through the challenge, and set a direction—one the team owns, together.

"If the team needs motivation, I challenge what they are doing, and
challenge the team to come up with solutions to elevate to the next
level. As the leader of the organization, I provide the broad vision and
communication to ensure everyone is working together. I try to demonstrate that as an organization, we are dependent on each other's talents

to succeed—and that with the right communication and teamwork, we will make the most of those talents.

"Like other Internet operations, our organization's most challenging moment came with the deflation of the Internet bubble. It was clear that the path we had been on required a radical change, that our broad approach needed focus, and that a new organization and direction were required.

"In my role as leader of the business, I needed to reinforce to everyone that major change was necessary. I pulled together a team of the right senior executives to set a vision for where we needed to be and to develop the restructuring plan and set the new direction.

"As the leader of the organization, my objective was not to develop and impose direction in isolation; my objective was to pull the team together to come to a solution using the knowledge and insight of the team.

"Only with input from a cross-section of the organization were we able to develop a very specific plan and direction, as well as critical business targets that became the rallying cry for the organization. By owning the outcome of that planning and restructuring effort, we all became bound to its success or failure. I believe that was a critical component of achieving a successful, on-schedule turnaround of our business to a profitable, high-growth operation.

"Teams are not democracies. Ask any football coach. Teams don't vote on which play to run or which strategy to pursue. The leader of the team ultimately has to make the decisions. In fact, the team or the business relies on the leader to make those decisions.

"However, in my approach to leading a team, I challenge the team to bring their experience, knowledge, and skills to the dialog. I want my team's collective wisdom to help guide the ultimate decision, but in the end that decision rests with one person.

"If it is a critical business or strategy decision for the entire business, then the ultimate decision maker is the leader of the business. By relying on the collective wisdom of the team, I believe I am more likely to make a better decision and the team is more likely to feel vested in the decision—even if I, as the leader, ultimately override the team's consensus.

"Through the dialog, the team will understand why I made the decision I made. Making decisions in isolation—without the dialog or input of the team—means the team is less likely to understand the reason for the decision and will be less likely to be vested in that decision.

"I work hard to make my team part of the process. I challenge them to bring their knowledge and experience to the process. I do that through extensive communication. If I am successful, the organization will fully understand our direction, they will feel and be part of it, they will think as a team and operate as a team, and we will be much more successful. It is a virtuous cycle.

"As the organization becomes more vested in our success and feels more responsible for our success, they will individually and collectively be more proactive about ensuring we are operating at our best. From that virtuous cycle comes the inherent leadership in a well-organized, focused team. Someone has to build and maintain that virtuous cycle, guide and direct that team, and make the ultimate decisions.

"If someone on the front lines of my organization has important insight and perspective that I can't have because of our relative roles, I want that person to feel free, or even compelled, to share that insight with the organization. Ultimately, I want that insight to have the opportunity to influence our decision making, if appropriate. Then, when a decision is made, if that insight played a role, I want that person on the front lines to know they made a difference.

"If that insight did not play a role, I want that person to understand why it didn't play a role so they can understand the decisions that are made. The only way this process works is if you have a well-organized team with very strong, efficient communication in place, and an understanding that the organization is an important part of the process.

"Listen to the feedback of your team to understand what your organization needs and where your leadership is needed. Fill in the voids, whatever they may be. Ensure there is direction and clarity, that the team understands that direction, and that every person in the organization understands their role in it. Listening guides your own actions, and communication, based on what you hear, guides the actions of the rest of the organization.

"Building and maintaining an organization that works in this way requires aggressive leadership—a vision for what needs to be achieved, a clear message about how the organization will operate, and the constant communication and guidance necessary to make it work. That must come from the leader of the organization.

"Leadership is an imperfect process that is never done, which creates the potential for frustration. Organizations continuously evolve and change, are continuously faced with new challenges to be met, and communication is complex and takes time. Understanding that the job is never done is key to maintaining focus and avoiding frustration and distraction. The organization needs to know that as well. Individuals can and will get frustrated and distracted, but as long as the team overall stays focused and its leaders stay focused, progress will be made.

"In many ways, leadership style is very personal. The best approach for anyone to take in a leadership role is the one that gets sustainable results for them. Finding the approach that works may require effort and time. I believe there is inherent leadership in people that is shaped by both personality and experience from birth. I also believe leadership can and needs to be developed. Whether a person has an inherently high level of leadership skills or not, anyone can and will develop better leadership capabilities through experience, maturity, and proactive development effort."

96

MICHAEL G. MEDZIGIAN, CEO

Watermark Capital Partners, LLC

Lead by example.

"Lead by example," advises Watermark's CEO, Michael Medzigian. "Expectations must be set very high in order for an organization to achieve and maintain world-class status.

"I don't believe that it is practical for a leader to set higher goals for others than he demands of himself. Excellence begets excellence! Part of the expectation that a leader should place on himself is a fluent understanding of subordinates' jobs—certainly with respect to all direct reports, and the deeper into the organization the better.

"I remember very early in my career the feeling of frustration associated with believing that I performed at a higher level than certain superiors. I suspect that this is a common dilemma for young, highly motivated people—sometimes accurate, but more often reflective of a lack of understanding of the superior's skills and duties, or of the knowledge that the superior would not or could not step into the subordinate's job duties.

"This is not about the fear associated with knowing that you are expendable and that others can fill your shoes. Rather, it is about the knowledge that others have a full appreciation of what you do, its complexities and its challenges. It is about the self-respect that comes with knowing that the boss thinks that what you do is sufficiently important, that somewhere during his career he took the time to learn it. Not just the concepts, but the details—any leader understands the concepts.

"Leaders can be categorized as big-picture strategic visionaries, detail-oriented operators, or a balance of the two. Even if you are the strategic visionary, you can't be visionary all the time, so sweat the small stuff in between—it pays dividends.

"A number of years ago I was recruited to be the CEO charged with turning around a troubled business. It was a challenging situation involving an organizational restructuring and the repositioning of existing investments. It was not hard to spot the 'him versus us' mentality while the staff sized me up and evaluated what agendas I brought with me and how they fit into my plans.

"Late one evening two junior staff members walked by my office, paused at the door and one of them said, 'partners don't work this late at night.' Having three young children at the time, I did not aspire to have it become a routine, but the needs of the business were such that long hours were the order of the day for me.

"I simply smiled, but as the days wore on and these junior associates found me regularly burning the midnight oil with them, increasingly open dialogue followed. Demonstrate that you are willing to get in the trenches. You will not only earn the respect of your team, you will be treated to a level of candor about the organization that typically only takes place over late night take out food in a conference room.

"The intention of working late was not to impress the staff. Being there late was a need of the business as I perceived it at the time. I do believe that a byproduct of being there late was an ability to get closer to the staff.

"I have always done everything in my power to ensure that organizations that I lead do not develop cultures that value face time. With that said, there can be nothing but good that comes from showing the rank and file that you are not above being there with them to accomplish something that is critical to the organization. It shows them the importance that is placed on what they do, and it shows them that things do not only flow one way.

"In the investment business, the Investment Committee meeting is where transaction professionals (and transaction teams) make presentations to the Investment Committee members (the Board) on a proposed investment, merger, or disposition. While the transaction team may simply present alternatives, they often advocate a specific strategy, and the dollars and associated risks and rewards can be enormous.

"A high-stakes meeting for everyone involved, the professional that is advocating the transaction and the analysts that have prepared the numbers and presentations are understandably uniquely exposed to both praise and criticism based on the quality of the analysis, the perceived quality of the transaction, and ultimately, the performance of the investment.

"Despite this, it is not uncommon to spot a leader that did not take the time to read the materials in advance of the meeting. While certainly acceptable, it is also common for a leader to form a conceptual notion about an investment and therefore not focus on the details of the presentation. Rather than simply reviewing these presentations in advance of the meetings, I also committed myself to the time necessary to learn the workings of the computerized models utilized by the analysts.

"It is not uncommon for young financial analysts with significant computer skills to view themselves as being better with numbers than their superiors. Similarly, not out of the ordinary for those of us who attended college prior to the introduction of the PC, I am generally more comfortable than today's analysts when it comes to doing mathematical equations in my head.

"Combining solid financial abilities with modeling fluency that is typically the domain of the analyst, I was better equipped than most others in the room to identify issues, errors, and alternative approaches. One result of course was improved work product and decision making.

"The other outcome was an increasingly close working relationship with the transaction teams. Rather than being viewed as the guy who approves or rejects the investments, I became a sort of sounding board regarding alternatives and issues being faced in the underwriting—exactly the position a leader wants to be in, and one that provides a unique window of understanding for any leader making investment decisions.

"I have to believe that there are leaders that excel who are lousy with details. We have certainly heard about the business partnerships where one person brings the vision but sufficiently respects the details so as to keep a high-level COO on the team.

"This may work in large organizations. But even in those instances, I think that you buy a tremendous amount of goodwill amongst associates, investors, competitors, and other outsiders when it is apparent that you have a tight grasp of the business.

"I have watched very smart leaders that had strong forward-thinking capabilities but who have been unable to lead due to their lack of interest in the details. It may work if one has a lack of interest, but does not have a lack of respect for the details. It does not work for me.

"We all bring different things to the dance. Some have pure intellectual horsepower. Some have superior educational or professional training. Some have multiple attributes. There are of course many who don't have the full package. I believe that sheer hard work can make up for other shortcomings and disadvantages. It may not sound enlightened, but I have seen it many times: hard work provides results.

"Always remember the things your parents taught you. Listen, lead by example, be empathetic, treat others within and outside the organization the way you want to be treated, always deliver on your commitments (do what you say you will do), there is no middle of the road when it comes to ethics, immerse yourself in all of the information that is available to you, and in those instances where you are not fully equipped, don't forgot the power of sheer hard work."

97

PETER H. SODERBERG, PRESIDENT AND CEO

Welch Allyn

I believe in a highly interactive, personal approach with employees and customers.

"I believe in a highly interactive, personal approach with employees and customers," says Peter Soderberg of medical equipment manufacturer, Welch Allyn. "This method utilizes one of my personal strengths, which is interpersonal communication, to paint the corporate vision. The way I communicate this vision is through a living, evolutionary presentation called Strategic Directions.

"It's the job of the CEO in a company like Welch Allyn, with real product breadth and diverse global markets, to knit the organization and its priorities together through common threads and a clear vision as to where we're headed. People are more engaged if they can relate their job to the broader purpose of our company. The more people hear the Welch Allyn vision and direction, the more they understand and relate to its purpose. The Strategic Directions presentation fits my leadership style because it provides a high-energy, open platform for dialogue.

"A few months ago we had a senior management meeting with the top leadership of one of the biggest hospital systems in the United States. We were fighting for a corporate-wide standardization of Welch Allyn equipment throughout all of their facilities. Our company was competing against two, very large multinational firms who took the approach of a 'whole hospital' turnkey system. Our team used the Strategic Directions presentation to focus on our core competencies, our award-winning products, and what we had on the drawing board for the future.

"The representatives from this hospital system saw our company as the best of breed supplier for a whole family of technologies to meet the demands of their user population. We offered products that reflected an appreciation for the unique clinical users of these sets of technologies in the spaces we targeted. It ended up that we were awarded the contract as a preferred supplier for this large hospital system.

"How did our team win this huge account? We articulated the Welch Allyn core values, we demonstrated our focus on technology, and we cemented the alignment of our company with their needs.

"There's no cookie cutter approach to what makes a great leader; it's really more like a fingerprint. A great leader melds their own personal strengths and compensates for their weaknesses with certain basics in leadership that are often learned.

"My education has come from studying the strengths and weaknesses of leaders I know personally, as well as those I read about. I prefer to learn by observation. I've evolved a style that helps me learn through continuous improvement. By watching others, I've realized how to mobilize and interact with my team to give them meaningful authority and capability to improve my productivity and effectiveness."

98

TYLER YOUNG, CEO
WF Young, Inc.
Constantly initiate change.

Strategic innovation is a hot topic today on the business seminar circuit, and many of the CEOs we interviewed, including Tyler Young of WF Young, Inc., rank innovation and change high on their list of priorities.

"My success as a leader has come about due to my ability to constantly initiate change," says Tyler. "Old companies need to reinvent themselves without losing their traditional values. The ability to push forward fresh initiatives has reaped significant benefit for my company."

WF Young is a 110-year-old family business. They have manufactured and marketed over-the-counter drugs and animal health care products over the company's history. They are best known for their consumer product, Absorbine Jr.

"Several years ago, I initiated a strategy to transition to a virtual marketing entity that relies on the outsourcing of products and services," explains Tyler.

A virtual marketing company uses outside resources to manufacture and distribute its products. Prior to forming the virtual company, WF Young manufactured 80 percent of its products. The company sells over 150 items in the human and animal health care industry. "We maintain a small staff to coordinate the efforts of outside services. Whenever possible, we outsource technology, service, and expertise. We retrained existing employees to empower them to focus on the needs of the customer and to work as a cohesive team.

"The current structure has enabled the company to transfer the use of its capital from work in process, raw materials, and equipment to brand acquisition and advertising support. Our sales have doubled and our expenses have been reduced."

Annual sales are in excess of $25 million, with the animal health care product line making up the majority share of revenues. "Absorbine Jr. is ranked number eight in market share in a crowded category dominated by Pfizer and several other large, multinational corporations. Our brand has greatly benefited by the renewed investment in new product introductions and continued advertising support."

An aggressive new product development program coupled with a series of acquisitions has contributed to WF Young's growth. Tyler is a fourth-generation member of the founding family.

Does a prejudice against nepotism adversely affect his company leadership? "In some companies, it can be difficult for a family member to command respect from long-term employees. My success came about due to my direct involvement working side-by-side with the rank and file throughout my career. I was taught to embrace humility and strive to champion the needs of the employees.

"The key executives who did not support me were carefully retired or terminated. There is no room in my organization for resistance to change. However, it can take a long time to cleanse a company of resistors. Terminations and a committed resolve to make a change earned respect among team members quickly.

"I have always treated people fairly, honestly, and compassionately while driving hard to accomplish goals. Our performance as a team has earned respect. Success breeds success. We are a very different type of organization today as we celebrate our 110th year of operation."

99

ANNE M. MULCAHY, CEO
Xerox Corporation
Get the cow out of the ditch.

The following is based on a speech that Xerox CEO, Anne Mulcahy, delivered to the Detroit Economic Club in September of 2002.

As Anne sees it, one of the most critical leadership skills is the ability to lead an organization out of a crisis and turn negatives into positives quickly.

"Xerox has been through a period of enormous crisis," says Anne. "But we're back, and getting stronger every day."

She says that as a new CEO, she got her best advice from a customer in Dallas, a prominent businessman who is active in civic and political life.

"He delighted in telling me that I reminded him of a farmer whose cow got stuck in a ditch." So she asked him what she could do about it. "He said, 'You've got to do three things. First, get the cow out of the ditch. Second, find out how the cow got in the ditch. Third, make sure you do whatever it takes so the cow doesn't get in the ditch again.'"

Mulcahy used this simple three-step process in leading Xerox's turnaround—although she found it helpful to reverse the first two steps, and understand first how Xerox got into trouble so she could better formulate a strategy for "getting the cow out of the ditch."

"In 1999 and early 2000, we attempted too much change too fast," she says. Competition stiffened, while economies at home and abroad weakened. Accounting improprieties in Mexico led the SEC to investigate Xerox, taking up a lot of precious management time. All of these and other problems—and some actions Mulcahy says were just plain "dumb"—hit Xerox simultaneously. And the cow fell into the ditch.

By May of 2002, Xerox was in deep trouble. Revenue and profits were declining. Cash on hand was shrinking. Debt was mounting. Customers were irate. Employees were defecting. And Xerox share price was cut in half.

Right around that time, Anne was promoted to president and COO of Xerox. Her immediate task: Get the cow out of the ditch—and make sure it doesn't stumble into the ditch again.

She and her team immediately laid out a recovery plan with three major components:

1. *Focus on cash generation to improve liquidity.* To increase liquidity, Xerox sold more than $2.5 billion in non-core assets, outsourced office manufacturing, and exited its small office/home office business. Operational cash generation was increased through disciplined management of inventory, receivables, and fixed capital. The company also entered into agreements with GE Capital and other sources to outsource the financing of customer receivables.

2. *Take $1 billion out of the cost base to improve competitiveness.* Xerox reduced inventory by about $600 million, a one-year improvement of 30 percent. Selling, general, and administrative costs were lowered by 15 percent. Capital spending was cut in half, and the workforce was trimmed by 15 percent worldwide. Total money taken out of the cost base: $1.3 billion.

3. *Strengthen the core businesses to ensure future growth.* About $1.6 billion was invested in R&D. In 2002, Xerox brought out more new products than any time in its history, including a third-generation color digital production publisher, new color multifunction office devices, and solutions and services in areas ranging from print-on-demand to book publishing.

What advice does Anne offer to other executives whose cows have fallen into the ditch?

"First look before you leap," she says. "There's a tendency to think you know all the answers. Take the precious time needed to truly understand the problems." Even though she has been with Xerox for over 25 years, when the crisis hit, Anne spent three months "settling the troops and understanding the problems."

Second, communicate. During the crisis, she did a dozen live television broadcasts for Xerox employees, conducted 80 town meetings, sent out 40 "letters to the troops," held hundreds of roundtables, and logged 200,000 miles visiting employees in more than a dozen countries.

"The response was overwhelming," she says. "Defections slowed to a trickle. Hope rekindled. Energy returned."

Ironically, being promoted during a business downturn actually worked to her advantage.

"Crisis is a powerful motivator. It enables you to do things you should have been doing all along. Whoever said that nothing focuses the mind like the sight of the gallows had it right."

She concludes: "Poor leadership can do serious damage virtually overnight. Good leadership—leadership that is consistent, honest, and forceful—can move mountains."

100

PETER A.J. GARDINER, CEO
Zindart, Ltd.

Perform or Go.

"After I got a few years of management under my belt, I developed an assessment tool I could take into any company. It revolved around asking three questions:

1. What business are we in?
2. What kind of organization do we need to execute?
3. What metrics should be used to monitor and measure our activities?

"With these three questions thoroughly answered, I could determine the strategic direction for the company and the structure needed to support it: the people it would require, a clear definition of responsibilities, the proper levels of authority, what monetary incentives would be offered to management, and the performance that would be required for success.

"All that was left would be to make sure the management team understood and embraced the marching order: POGO, or 'Perform Or GO.'

"POGO gives top executives a clear direction, goals, and incentives. They've helped me outline the tools they'll need, they now have a clear outline of their responsibilities, and they know they can get help from the CEO when they need it. If you choose the right group, they put their heads down and get on with it.

"After all, POGO applies not only to the management team but to the CEO. In fact, in every case, I was first in line. If I couldn't meet the performance goals we'd agreed on to turnaround the company, the board of directors, in each case, would have expected me to resign, to perform or go.

"For the last decade, the academic gurus from American business schools have been espousing *collaboration* and *teamwork*—a more humanized approach. Those concepts are all fine and good, but I wonder if the flip-flop to such a soft approach is going to produce a couple of generations of managers who will settle for less performance.

"As a British-born executive who chose to become a naturalized citizen of the U.S., I think we need to think twice about whether what seems to me to be a total focus on including everyone in the decision can really deliver what made us a great nation after World War II.

"As a matter of fact, a half dozen hot sellers on Amazon.com's business book list say we need to move back to the basics in turning around and running businesses. I would say Matthew J. Cullian has hit it on the head with his tome, *Back to Basics Management: The Lost Craft of Leadership*. The scale may have, in recent years, tipped too far toward 'discussion.'

"Associated British Maltsters (ABM) was a public company. I was put in charge of running it after it was acquired by Dalgety, the largest agribusiness company in Europe. At the time, ABM was the largest producer of malt in the U.K., but had only modest sales outside Britain. Malt is the basic ingredient for whisky, beer, and dozens of other grain-based products, such as Ovaltine.

"It was at ABM that I first developed the management concept that I came to call POGO. When I arrived at ABM, the company was in deep trouble. During my tenure as Managing Director—the equivalent of CEO in the U.S.—ABM became the second largest malting company in the world. We did it by bringing our operational cost structure down, using the performance indices appropriate for malting; expanding the company's sales and marketing staff; and aggressively seeking new geographic and industry markets for the company's products.

"In this case, we decided ABM's real opportunity was in expanding our exports. We focused on finding overseas markets and sought out new industries that could use the raw materials we produced. As a result, the company won the prestigious Queens Award for Export Achievements.

"By the time I left ABM to become CEO of Dalgety USA, the company had become the leading international maltster, supplying 70 percent of the ingredients for the Scotch whisky industry and a significant portion of the malt for brewing and several food categories worldwide. In two years, we doubled revenues and improved profitability by 700 percent.

"ABM was later acquired by Paul's Malt and then another company, and doesn't exist as a brand any more.

"My next assignment was to grow Dalgety, Inc., the American arm of Dalgety. At the time, Dalgety, Inc., was in the commodity business, with interests in fish, steel, grain byproducts, property, shipping, and seeds and pulses. It also had an interest in frozen vegetables. The whole region was doing only $90 million in sales and operating at a $6 million loss, annually.

"My first activity was to remove the management team that was in place, create a new team, and work through the principles of POGO—deciding what business we were in or wanted to be in, what organizational structure and tools we needed, what performance indices would produce the results we were seeking, and how management would be compensated if we got there.

"In six months, we were all agreed—it was clear we needed to take the company in a new direction.

"Over the next three years, we sold off the commodity businesses, grew the frozen division into the #1 position in the world, and moved Dalgety into the food distribution, additive, and coatings business, acquiring several companies along the way.

"Later we moved into fresh vegetables and, as the industry evolved, were the first company to get into prewashed, longlife packaged fresh vegetables, which are now standard provisions for the retail grocery industry and an approximately $2.5 billion market.

"Over the sixteen years I spent at Dalgety, POGO helped me take the young U.S. division from $90 million in sales to more than $4.6 billion, half of the company's worldwide sales.

"When I came out of retirement and took a position as CEO at Zindart, Ltd. in 2001, I faced another turnaround. The three operating divisions of this Hong Kong-based manufacturer were all underperforming.

"One of the first steps I undertook was the elimination of the top management group and the creation of a group structure with three independent operating units: Corgi, Hua Yang, and Zindart Manufacturing, each headed by an experienced, take-charge CEO tasked with the responsibility of energizing his individual organization.

"Over the next six months, all three units worked with me to put in new controls, reduce overhead, and eliminate inefficiencies. Our operations in Hong Kong were reorganized and upgraded, resulting in substantial improvements in worker productivity.

"Both our specialty printing unit, Hua Yang, and our manufacturing division, Zindart Manufacturing, wrote new strategic plans calling for diversifying their product offerings to attract customers in new industry segments, and the development of sales operations in new geographic markets. And both division CEOs helped set the performance indices for their line of business.

"Meanwhile, our brand name operating unit, Corgi Classics, with an entirely different business plan, charged ahead. Corgi has always been a well-regarded consumer brand in the die-cast vehicles collectible market, holding a leadership position in the UK.

"But until two years ago, Corgi had only limited sales, distribution, and consumer following in the U.S. We quickly began a two-pronged strategy—expansion of our distribution in the big American market coupled with new marketing initiatives, including the introduction of several lines of new product specifically designed to interest the American consumer.

"By the end of fiscal 2002, our second year of operation, Corgi had expanded to 600 direct accounts selling our new U.S. collector series, and another approximately 400 accounts served by wholesalers and rep groups. Corgi had also added FAO Schwartz, the finest toy specialty retailer in the U.S.

"One of the reasons was Corgi's new 'Unsung Heroes,' a range of meticulously researched, precision-engineered military vehicles—helicopters, battle tanks, personnel carriers, and utility trucks—replicating the exact equipment used by the U.S. military in the Vietnam War, accompanied by the story of a real soldier who operated one of those units in the war.

"Our final area of attack for Corgi has been the mass market. It's starting to pay off.

"Meanwhile, with increasing revenues, we have worked to steadily reduce term debt from U.S. $30 million in mid-1999 to U.S. $7 million at the end of fiscal 2002. Our report to shareholders for 2003 will show revenue increases in all three units, while overhead has been reduced, and the best profit margins yet, together with further reductions in term debt.

"In just two years, applying POGO leadership performance tools has boosted the market cap of Zindart, Ltd. from $9 million to $60 million."

THE TOP 15 LEADERSHIP STRATEGIES OF THE WORLD'S MOST SUCCESSFUL CEOS

1. Have a clear vision, a specific direction, and a goal for your organization.
2. Focus on the two or three things most important to your vision and goals. Don't spread your attention too thin.
3. Communicate your vision, strategy, goals, and mission to everyone involved—senior management, employees, suppliers, vendors, customers, shareholders, and other stakeholders.
4. Listen to what others tell you. Be willing to accept and act upon criticism and suggestions.
5. Surround yourself with the right people, a strong team.
6. Treat your employees exceedingly well. Help them become successful in their careers and their lives.
7. Apply the Golden Rule: Do unto others as you would have others do unto you.
8. Be in a business you love and are passionate about.
9. Constantly innovate to gain and sustain competitive advantage and serve your customers better.
10. Plan everything. Leave nothing to chance.
11. Be a leader and actually *lead*. Take responsibility. Make tough decisions.
12. Lead by example. Don't expect your people to do what you won't or don't do yourself.
13. Listen to the people who are closest to the customers and the marketplace. They will give you your best advice and input.
14. Set performance goals and establish metrics by which you can measure your performance and results.
15. Be service-oriented. How can you make the lives of your employees and customers better, easier, and more rewarding?

BOOKS

The Leadership Engine by Noel Tichy.

The Leadership Challenge by James Kouzes and Barry Posner (Josey-Bass, 2002, hardcover, 496 pages, $27.95)

The 21 Indispensable Qualities of a Leader by John Maxwell (Thomas Nelson, 1999, hardcover, 157 pages, $17.99)

Leadership by Rudolph Giuliani (Miramax, 2002, hardcover, 407 pages, $25)

More Than a Pink Cadillac: Mary Kay, Inc.'s Nine Leadership Keys to Success by Jim Underwood (McGraw-Hill, 2002, hardcover, 204 pages, $21.95)

PERIODICALS

Executive Leadership, monthly newsletter published by Newsletter Holdings, 703-905-8000.

Leadership, monthly newsletter published by Ragan Communications, 773-975-5020.

Leadership Strategies, monthly newsletter published by Briefings Publishing Group, 800-722-9221.

SCHOOLS/CENTERS

The Center for Creative Leadership in Greensboro, NC (http://www.ccl.org/index.shtml)

William F. Achtmyer Center for Global Leadership (School of Business at Dartmouth) (http://mba.tuck.dartmouth.edu/cgl/index.html)

Center For Career and Leadership Development (http://www.calumet.purdue.edu/ccld/)

At Yale School of Management, the Chief Executive Leadership Institute (http://www.ceoleadership.com/conferences/previous/yale percent202001/list.html)

Graduate Program in Leadership at Trinity (http://www.twu.ca/Leadership/)

The James MacGregor Burns Academy of Leadership (http://www.academy.umd.edu/ila/governing.htm)

U Penn Lessons in Leadership Forum (http://www.sas.upenn.edu/fox leadership/reg/event_index.php?P=1)

Boston College—The Center for Responsible Leadership (http://www.bc.edu/schools/csom/leadership/)

CEO Program at The Leadership (in Maryland) (http://www.theleader ship.org/CEOProgram/CEOProgram.asp) Wharton Leadership Courses (http://leadership.wharton.upenn.edu/l_change/courses.shtml)

Leader to Leader Foundation (formerly the Drucker Foundation) (http://drucker.org/leaderbooks/index.html)

Stanley K. Lacy Leadership Association (http://www.sklla.org/)

National Leadership Institute at the University of Maryland (http://www.umuc.edu/nli/mkting/market5.html)

FORUMS

Chamber Executive's Leadership Forum (July 2003) (http://www.us chamber.com/chambers/programs/elf/default.htm)

BusinessWeek CEO Leadership Forums: In Cooperation with America's best B-schools (http://conferences.businessweek.com)

TEC. TEC is a vital personal and professional development resource for thousands of the world's most successful CEOs. With more than 7,000 members in fourteen countries on six continents, TEC is widely recognized as *the* preeminent organization for CEOs in the world. (http://www.executive-roundtables.com)

World Economic Forum Annual Leadership Meeting (http://www.we forum.org/site/homepublic.nsf/Content/Annual+Meeting+2003)

Illinois Institue of Technology Business Leadership Forum (http://www.stuart.iit.edu/ceo_series.html)

WEB SITES

About motivation/leadership (http://www.themotivationalspeaker.com /leadershipstyles/, http://www.manyworlds.com)

The CEO Refresher (http://www.refresher.com/ceo.html)

CEO Support.com. CEO Support Systems, Inc.'s unique portfolio of resources is designed specifically for CEOs, presidents, and owners of small- and medium-sized businesses that are committed to growing their companies and themselves. Under the umbrella of Blueprint for a Healthy Organization, CEO Support Systems successfully delivers a powerful, yet simple and affordable way to help CEOs build value. (http://www.ceosupport.com)

Chief Executives Working Together (http://www.tec-best-practices .com)

The Federal Executive Institute and Management Development Centers (http://www.leadership.opm.gov, http://leadershipdecision works.com)

CEOs for Cities convenes mayors, corporate executives, university presidents, and other nonprofit leaders to share best practices in economic competitiveness and to design strategies to promote those practices. Leaders are typically recruited in clusters, forming member cities, though several serve as at-large members. (http://www .ceosforcities.org/network/index.html)

Chief executive coaching, development and leadership training for professionals committed to business and personal growth, offering peer group mentoring and information exchange environments. (http://www.excellceo.com, http://www.venturecoach.com)

Eric Yaverbaum is president of Jericho Communications, a New York public relations firm that has represented IKEA, Domino's Pizza, Bell Atlantic, American Express, Hain Celestial Group, Prince Tennis, Sony, Progressive Auto Insurance, Estee Lauder, Subway Sandwiches, Jose Cuervo, EMI Music, Billy Blanks, Goldfish Colors, H&M Clothing, and Camp Beverly Hills Clothing. Jericho has won numerous awards for its PR work, including a Big Apple Award, Bronze Anvil Certificate, and numerous CIPRAs (Creativity in Public Relations awards).

Eric is the author of *I'll Get Back to You* (McGraw-Hill) and *Public Relations Kit for Dummies* (IDG). He is a regular on the lecture circuit, speaking to professional organizations across the country on the art of public relations. His appearances on national and regional television and radio programs include *CBS This Morning, The Today Show,* CNN, *Larry King Live,* Bloomberg Radio, Fox Broadcasting's *Fox & Friends,* NPR, CNN, Book Nook, Associated Press Radio, and *WFAM Morning Magazine.*

A graduate of The American University, Eric is an active member of the Young President's Organization and the Public Relations Society of America. He volunteers his time to the Multiple Sclerosis Society and fundraisers for cancer.

Share the message!

Bulk discounts
Discounts start at only 10 copies. Save up to 55% off retail price.

Custom publishing
Private label a cover with your organization's name and logo. Or, tailor information to your needs with a custom pamphlet that highlights specific chapters.

Ancillaries
Workshop outlines, videos, and other products are available on select titles.

Dynamic speakers
Engaging authors are available to share their expertise and insight at your event.

**Call Dearborn Trade Special Sales at 1-800-245-BOOK (2665)
or e-mail trade@dearborn.com**

Dearborn™
Trade Publishing
A **Kaplan Professional** Company